A City Set On A Hill

The Courage To Be Seen

Shamina Allen

outskirtspress

DENVER, COLORADO

God grant me the serenity to accept the things
I cannot change; courage to change the things I can;
and wisdom to know the difference. Living one day
at a time; Enjoying one moment at a time; Accepting
hardships as the pathway to peace; Taking, as He
did, this sinful world as it is, not as I would have it;
Trusting that He will make all things right if I
surrender to His Will; That I may be reasonably
happy in this life and supremely happy with
Him Forever in the next. Amen.
--Reinhold Niebuhr

Dedicated to:
All the wild flowers and the roots that keep them
grounded. God hasn't forgotten you.

Introduction

A City Set on a Hill...

IF I'VE KNOWN nothing else in my thirty years on this earth, I can say I know what it's like to lose. I know what it's like to lose hope, to lose your faith, to lose your mind, to lose time, love, and direction. Losing, by definition, means to be deprived of or to cease to have or retain something. I can stomach losing because it doesn't discredit your faith or your efforts, but giving up is perhaps one of the hardest things I ever had to do. To be willing to admit that the odds are against me, to accept the probability of defeat; that is what I just can't digest. The hardest part about giving up is that it doesn't necessarily mean the thing you're giving up ever belonged to you at all; it simply means you stopped pursuing it in the face of overwhelming opposition.

It wasn't until recently that God revealed to me that in order to gain the blessings of Christ, I had to lose some things and give up some things. I thank God for showing me that giving up is not always a sign of defeat, but rather a demonstration of obedience.

E was the total opposite of me. He was fearless and appeared to be so free; I saw so much life in him, the life I was too scared to have for myself. We were married for three years, and in that time I experienced the presence of God and came face to face with the devil.

Many nights we would sit and talk about our wedding

day, how the church seemed to have been filled with a thick white mist, like the angels had walked the aisles all night. I had no clue what I was in for; I trusted him with my life and I almost lost it all.

I married a man whom I knew to have had a homosexual experience. This was not your typical down-low experience; there were no secrets, or so I thought. I loved him on purpose, flaws and all. I had no idea spiritually and naturally what I was up against. My ex-husband not only enjoyed sex with other men, he also had a desire to live his life as a transsexual. His knowledge of women and what he thought it meant to be a grown woman tortured me throughout our entire marriage.

E had his own vision of what women should be, and I had no idea who I was. I was a blank canvas and he was an artist. For so long, I lived with the shame and embarrassment of what many would call a failed marriage, but as my story unfolds I realize my marriage could never have been a failure, because it did everything but fail. It is responsible for catapulting me into my destiny, and for that reason I am grateful. The truth is, E was only half of my problems.

My struggles began long before I met E and long before I even existed. It was a tradition of hopelessness and defeat that was passed down to me like a treasured family heirloom. Its roots run deep in the foundations of my family, carried down generations from mother to daughter. My greatest battle would be figuring out how to get rid of it.

CHAPTER 1

The Family Heirloom

"Listen! A sower went out to sow. And as he sowed, some seed fell along the path, and the birds came and devoured it. Other seed fell on rocky ground, where it did not have much soil, and immediately it sprang up, since it had no depth of soil. And when the sun rose, it was scorched, and since it had no root, it withered away. Other seeds fell among thorns, and the thorns grew up and choked it, and it yielded no grain. And other seeds fell into good soil and produced grain, growing up and increasing and yielding thirtyfold and sixtyfold and a hundredfold." - Mark 4:3-8, (KJV)

CONTRARY TO WHAT many may believe, I didn't come from a praying, God-fearing family at all. I didn't have a praying, fasting grandmother, on whose lap I could just lay my head and cry, while she poured into me her life's wisdom. I never knew my grandmother, but I heard stories about her -- or rather, pieces of stories. Eventually, I began to come up with my own conclusions about her. I imagined her as a warm and nurturing woman who loved to bake.

When I was little, I would tell myself if she were here, everything would be different, but the truth is she was far from the grandmother I envisioned.

Her name was Elizabeth, and she was a tall, slender woman with a personality that could light up a room. She was so vibrant and had a smile that just couldn't be contained. Judging by her pictures, she was a noticeably gorgeous woman. I remember looking at an old class picture of her that my mother kept in a small photo album. She wore a scarf tied around her neck with the bow flared out to the left side, with the collar of her white shirt flipped up and one hand on her hip. When I first saw the picture I couldn't help but stare at her smile; it was subtle and sassy all at the same time. She had beautiful long black wavy hair, and at first glance you would think she was a white woman. She had that timeless beauty that I imagined was very popular amongst the men, my grandfather being one of them.

He was a tall man, about six feet four inches, from what I've been told. He was a handsome man, but he knew it, and he wasn't a stranger to spreading his love around. He had seven children by four different women, including my grandmother. Although I imagine my grandfather was a handful with all the women he entertained, I always felt in my heart that it was my grandmother who got the worst of him. He was a heavy alcoholic and was drunk more than he was sober. My mother would tell me about how he would beat my grandmother so badly she thought he was going to kill her.

My mother told me how life was in the house with my grandmother and grandfather; how she watched her mother wither away at the hands of my grandfather and the drinking.

It all just sucked the life right out of my grandmother, day after day, until she was just a fraction of who she used to be. Her smiles and sense of humor turned into drunken slurs of bitterness -- yet, my grandmother never left my grandfather. You can imagine what life for my mother was like. I remember her telling me stories about how she had no shoes and no food. I have heard stories about the winters where she would come home in tears with her hands red and stiff from the cold, and no gloves to keep her warm.

Besides my grandmother's inability to provide the bare necessities, she was not the best mother and, often consumed by her own life, she frequently left my mother alone. Being the only girl in a dysfunctional family of men was never safe, and as a result my mother was a victim of molestation. Lost and without guidance, my mother stumbled through the years of her youth trying to cling to my grandmother, who was broken and weary. Eventually, all the drinking got the best of my grandmother and at thirty-six years old she died from cirrhosis of the liver; my mother was nine years old at the time. My grandfather died shortly after from a heart attack.

My mother and her brothers were taken in by my great-grandmother in an attempt to honor her daughter's dying wishes. My great-grandmother was so broken-hearted to have her daughter die before herself that she ruled over my mother with an iron fist, trying to protect her from the world and hoping to prevent her from falling into the same fate as her mother -- but somehow my mother met my father, George Kenny.

They met through a mutual friend. My mother's best friend was dating my father's best friend at the time, and suggested that the two of them meet. It was only a matter of time before they began a relationship. My mother was only sixteen years old at the time, and my father was twenty-three. Less than a year after their meeting, my mother became pregnant, and reality started to set in. My great-grandmother was not happy, to say the least, but she always tried to keep my mother close, so she allowed my father to practically move into her house just to keep my mother close. However, she was no pushover, and it was only a matter of time before my father couldn't take any more of her constant meddling in their relationship, and he quickly moved my mother out of my great-grandmother's house and into a one-bedroom apartment on the other side of town.

Without the direction of my grandmother, my mother was like a caged bird set free -- she had no idea what life in the real world was like. My father was very controlling and he wanted nothing more than to have my mother home, where he felt she belonged. He wasn't cruel, but rather selfish; he took care of everything and my mother was truly able to trust that he would take care of her -- but at the cost of dealing with his drug habit, his temper, and his rules that involved her rarely visiting family or having any outside life that didn't include him.

Yet through all the stress and the confusion, on May 9, 1981 something changed for the next generation of women in the family: something shifted in the spiritual realm and in the earth that would never be the same again. My mother, at the age of seventeen, rushed to the hospital that night to fulfill her purpose. As she lay there in the cold, sterile delivery room, she pushed and travailed, being only a child herself. Her perseverance made a declaration in the atmosphere that the generational curse of defeat and hopelessness that had plagued the women of our family for years would be destroyed. With the last of her energy she pushed and travailed, but through her veins she still passed on the family heirloom containing the despair, the abuse, and the addictions -- but along with it, she managed to give me everything needed to destroy it. Scared and tired, she gave me every inch of herself on that delivery table: her will, her endurance, and her courage to try. It had to have been somewhere between the intense groans of pain that I believe God found favor in her — in us.

Realizing that she could never stop what this life would take me through, all the trials and tribulations I would have to face, God interceded on my behalf and at that crucial moment God spoke a word of life into my destiny: that I would not have to be bound by addiction, fear, and abuse, but that I could live an abundant life and have peace. On May 9, 1981 at 3 o'clock a.m. my mother gave birth to a five-pound, thirteen-ounce baby girl, and a promise that would change everything. As for me, that was the first day of the rest of my life and the beginning of the fiercest battle I would ever have to face: the fight to protect my destiny.

CHAPTER 2

Too Much, Too Little

MY FATHER NAMED me Shamina. I was born in the concrete maze of the Bronx, in New York, where few manage to find their way out. I am the firstborn of my mother Cheryl Allen and my father, George Kenny. Ironically, I would be the first to accomplish many things in my life, but not without a price to pay. Bound by fear and worry, I carried a heavy load. My mother and my father were addicts, like many of the parents during that time, who were either strung-out addicts on crack, or alcoholics. I call them victims of the New Jack City era that tore families apart and left eighties babies like me to take the fall.

I remember hearing a story in the Bible about a man named David who killed a giant with just a sling. I was told that the giant represents anything in your life that tries to stop you from achieving your destiny. At a young age I realized I wasn't as fortunate as David. I had to slay my Goliath without a sling, and it was no easy task. The giants in my life seemed to multiply. Just as one would fall, another would come and take its place. The giants in my life were massive and ruthless -- they blocked out the sun and all signs of hope; they showed no mercy, and at times seemed impossible to face.

In order to survive, I had to learn quickly what took some adults a lifetime to grasp. I got real good at keeping secrets from friends, and some family. The family secret had to be protected. No one could know what was going on inside Apartment 6C of 1428 Webster Avenue. The slightest word slipping out by mistake could mean never seeing my sisters and brothers again. I promised them we wouldn't have to go through foster care for as long as I could help it. So I became solid as a rock, never letting anyone get past a certain level of emotion with me. I knew if they could tap into me—the real me screaming for help on the inside— then the secrets would pour out of me like lava. So I became an observer, never quick to speak, analyzing everything and everyone around me. Ironically, it was this same talent that would later keep me in bondage.

I was a bold child, mature beyond my years, capable of dealing with issues that others would think were impossible. I was a daddy's girl, stuck to him like glue. I was his princess and he was everything to me. I felt so safe when he was around. He worked so hard to preserve my innocence, that I would see no evil. I discovered later, when I was a little older, that my father was also an addict, and he was responsible for introducing my mother to drugs -- he was just better at it than my mother. He was what you would call a functional addict. He was able to maintain his habit and still keep a clean house, cook, and he wasn't too bad of a hairdresser to me and my sister. Sometimes I still laugh about the sponge rollers on Easter. It took two days for our bangs to drop the tight curls floating in the front of our heads. I remember Christmases filled with the sounds of Motown Christmas records, the whole house draped in Christmas lights, presents spilling over from under a six-foot Christmas tree. Even when things were bad, he had a way of keeping it together. I loved waking up to the smell of Pine-Sol and the sound of soul classics. We always had music. It was a must to have surround-sound speakers spread throughout the entire house. Those were the good old days.

I adored my father, and although I could never understand what kind of man he was to my mother, the saddest day of my life was when he moved out. It was late; I sat in my room stretched out over my bed, looking through the window bars at the streetlights' beams off the side of the project buildings, when I heard a loud crash. It sounded like glass breaking and voices screaming. I never slept very hard, so I was always the first or only one up to see things like this. I remember jumping out of my bed and peeking through the crack of my bedroom door, when I heard my mother shouting and my father screaming back to her, "I'm leaving!" At that moment I ran into the room screaming, "Stop!" and begging my father not to leave as he rushed to his room with a black plastic bag, filling it with his things. It all happened so fast. I didn't know why they were fighting or what was happening. All I knew was that I felt a sudden tear on the inside, my heart being ripped out of me and shoved in a black plastic bag and thrown over my father's shoulder as he made his way to the front door. At that moment, I didn't care what they were fighting about, but I knew what I was fighting for. I screamed from the deepest place in me, "Daddy, NO! Don't leave me, please!" I fell to the floor with my eyes swollen from my tears as I grabbed for his leg, dragging myself to the front door with him. "Please don't leave me here!" I just knew that if my father saw me in such desperation, his princess, scraping her knees on the floor trying to keep hold of his jeans, he would turn around and hold me in his arms and stay. But he left. My soul shook as the heavy metal door slammed behind him.

I ran to my window, where I would usually watch the streetlights hit the sides of the building, but tonight all I could see was the streetlights hit the empty, hard black concrete. I waited to see if Daddy was going to walk past. And for a minute I saw him with his bag over his shoulder walking past my window. I screamed, "Come back! Daddy! Daddy!" but he never turned around. After a few steps I lost sight of him. Suddenly, I hated those window bars because I couldn't stick my head out the window to see him walk up the block. I felt like there was something more I could have done to make him stay—if only he could have seen my face one more time, if I could just fit my head out the window, then he would have turned around. But I was trapped in those damn metal bars like an animal, my face pressed up against the cold metal rods, hoping my father would save me.

Life for my siblings and me was never quite the same after my father left. The house rarely stayed clean, and instead of coming home from school to the sound of the Chi-Lites singing "I do love you," we were greeted by a cold, bitter quiet that made the night that much harder. I got held back in the first grade because of my attendance. It was so hard for my mother to get into the swing of doing all the things my father used to do. He took care of a lot when it came to us. I knew my mother was lost being all alone. My father was the kind of man who wanted to keep her in a box for himself. His only requirement was that she sit pretty in her box, and he would take care of everything else, which hurt my mother in the long run. So when he left I stepped up and carried the load, while my mother did what she knew best: she went on a quest to find refuge in the arms of any man willing to take on the challenge of providing for us, or at least making life easier for her to stand.

She loved us with every bit of her soul, but the harsh reality is that she struggled with the responsibility of being a mother. When my father was gone I watched something in her shift, and the reality of being a single mother never rested well with her. Relationship after relationship, I watched as my mother lost herself in every available bachelor who showed interest. One after the other, we dated them right alongside her and she never even noticed. One after the other, they would disappear. No one lasted long enough for us to get close to them -- and truth be told, we were like a fort, and it wasn't easy to penetrate through our alliance to my father. Yet secretly, just like my mother, there were times when we actually hoped some of them were different from the rest. We hoped that her knight in shining armor would come and stitch up all the open wounds we all had and possibly be the Cosby dad I had always wanted. I wanted her to be happy in love—she was so much better that way—but I also could never sit back and allow some fly-by-night loser to come in and try to rule over her and play daddy for a few months with us. It was for that reason that my mom and I had such a rough time in our relationship during my adolescent years.

And what did my father have to say about these fly-by-night relationships? As for our father, we didn't see him much after he left. He started dating a woman with four kids of her own; her children were no more than a year apart from us, and some were the same age. It was weird. I always thought to myself that he missed us so much he tried to find a family to replace us. Over time I began to discover that my superhero was nothing more than a man. He would make promises to pick us up and let us spend the night with him, but when he did show up, he always had an excuse why we couldn't go with him, and I always accepted them willingly. I knew he was lying, but I never wanted to ruin the image of him in my mind. I wanted him to lie to me, to give me something to believe in. During one of his visits he told me that he was going to come home one day, and he and my mother were going to get back together. He said it so much that it became his introduction to every lie. I do still remember the time he promised to take us all to Disney World, and for some reason I believed him -- or at least I wanted to believe him. So I would wait, day after day, for him to come home and take us to Disney World, but one afternoon, about five years after he moved out, I stopped waiting. That was the day my father was murdered.

I was ten years old when it happened. He had been shot by a sixteen-year-old kid from his neighborhood over a basketball game and a twenty-dollar bet. It was never in my father's nature to turn down an opportunity to earn some extra money. He was known amongst the neighborhood for his skills in basketball, so he thought it would be easy money. He won and lost at the same time, and that was one game I wish he hadn't had to play. My siblings and I found out one afternoon after school. My mother sat us down in the living room and told us Daddy had been in an accident and he was hurt. We asked if he was okay, and the look on her face said it all. "No, he's not okay, babies; he's gone." The world stood still, and in that moment hopes and dreams died. I was suffocating in my own sorrow. I remember that eerie silence that fell on the room. All I could hear was the sound of my heavy breathing, short and quick, trying to catch my breath. We all felt the thinness, as if the air was being sucked out of the room. Hearts aching in our chest, nauseous, dizzy -- something was taken from each of us that day, and there was nothing I could do.

CHAPTER 3

Survival

AFTER MY FATHER died, I believe it was then that I developed terrible anxiety. It was almost immediately after he left that the nightmares and the vomiting started. It was like clockwork. I would wake up in a cold sweat, and every morning I would have to vomit in order to face the day.

The nightmares were never the same; but I will never forget my first one:

It's early in the day. The sun is shining so bright you can hardly see from the glare. I am standing in the middle of a playground. I am surrounded by the children laughing and playing around me. I can smell the damp concrete from the sprinklers across the park; I hear the children screaming in delight. I can feel their joy -- it feels so good; it's so compelling...it makes me want to smile. I stand there watching them play until I can no longer contain myself; their joy consumes me and paints a smile on my face from ear to ear. As I smile they seem to all turn and look at me with excitement as they each begin to yell, "Come and play with us!" "Yeah, Come on!" I feel like running over and joining them, but just as I get up enough courage to move, my eyes are drawn to the far end of the park where there's nothing but trees and grass and him; a blurred figure of a man watching me. He never moves or attempts to come toward me, but his presence I can't ignore. Instantly the joyful sound of the children playing becomes faint and it almost seems to disappear; the feeling of joy is replaced by an overwhelming fear that paralyzes me, and my smile transforms into an intense stare. The figure of the man is so far that I can't make out his face at all, but I can feel his presence as if he were standing right next to me. My heart is beating so fast that I think it's going to burst right out of my chest. I can't speak or move, but I can hear him breathing heavily. I am so scared that I can't stand it anymore and I open my eyes, with my heart still pounding in my chest, just to find myself lying in my dark bedroom.

I remember looking over to see if my sister was in the bed beside me; when I saw her, I could be sure I wasn't dreaming anymore. I remember the sigh of relief as I wrapped myself up in my bed sheets, leaving just a small opening for a view of the entire bedroom. I spent many nights being the only one up during the late hours of the night due to my nightmares. I would stare at my bedroom from wall to wall for hours until eventually I would begin to image how my room would look if I had the money to decorate it the way I wanted. I was in love with purple back then, so I would envision lavender walls with beautiful purple ruffle curtains hanging from the windows, and a dresser topped with dolls and stuffed animals. My favorite part was to imagine the most beautiful matching bedding set for me and my sister, but after about an hour of imagining I slowly drifted back to reality, as I glanced again at my little sister's bed covered in faded sheets that barely fit the stained mattress she slept on.

I couldn't help but notice the bare windows with nothing on them but old beige plastic shades that had been there since we moved in. I'd stare at our clothes packed into overflowing black trash bags, all of which were shoved into a closet with the door dangling from its hinges. There was nothing bright or girly about my room; it often felt cold and bare. I never understood how a decorated room could mean so much to a little girl, how the colors could inspire her and the smell of fresh sheets could comfort her, but it was the one thing I constantly wanted to change. It meant a lot to me to have one place, someplace that was perfect just for me, where I could be comfortable. It was hard to dream in my room -- there was no inspiration to be found in the cracks on the walls, so I created a fantasy world in my head and a longing in my heart to one day make those fantasies a reality.

Aside from the nightmares, things only got worse after my father died. I became a survivor accustomed to doing much with little. There was never a consistent routine in my mother's house; every day was a gamble. It wasn't hard to notice the difference in my world compared to the lives of others my age. I found it so hard to relate to anything they were feeling or going through. My life was so much more complicated. I can remember washing out my brothers' and sisters' clothing with Ivory soap in the bathroom sink for school; I remember trying to make a meal out of flour, water, and peanut butter.

I can never forget the day I thought I was going to lose it. I was so tired that day, just emotionally and physically tired.

On my way home from picking everybody up from school, I remember praying that by some chance my mother would be awake and would have some dinner ready when we got home, but as I arrived home the smells of roach spray and stale laundry were all that was there to greet me. My mother was locked in her room asleep, as she normally was. I was so angry. I rushed in the house, dropped my book bag on the floor, and went straight to her room. I banged on the door as hard as I could, shouting, "Ma! What are we going to eat! There's no food in here! Ma! Open the door!" But I could hear her snoring, and I knew she wasn't going to get up. I stood at the door for five minutes after I stopped knocking and I just wanted to scream and rip the door down, but I knew it wasn't going to make a difference. I was on my own and I had to figure it out. My stomach was hurting so bad; the school lunch had worn off and we were all hungry.

I started my siblings with their homework and I walked into the kitchen. I opened each cabinet to see what we had that could possibly feed us all. I found a bag of flour and a jar of peanut butter that we had received some time ago from a free food truck that was parked outside of the projects. I placed my hand on the sink and hung my head down, taking a deep breath. I had to push past the hunger pains, the sorrow I felt -- and I had to make it work. As I lifted my head, I went into survival mode. I looked in the refrigerator hoping to find something to help me make sense of the flour, but there was nothing, so I got a bowl and poured the flour into it and added some water. I rolled it together until I had a big glob of dough; then I began to take pieces of the dough and twist them like crescent rolls, hoping to make them seem a little more appealing to my brothers and sister.

When it was done I put the biscuits on a plate with peanut butter in the middle, and we all sat at the table and prayed over our food.

I was so nervous that they wouldn't eat it, but they smiled at the neatly rolled crescent shapes and began to dip them in the peanut butter. I made so many that they ate until they were full. At the end of the night I could hear them walking to their rooms talking about how good the biscuits were and in that moment, I knew there was nothing I wouldn't do for them, nothing I wouldn't face for them. I was the one person they could depend on, and I didn't take that lightly.

Once they were in bed I would pull out any leftover portions that I managed to save and pick the lock of my mother's room. I would bring her water and attempt to feed her. She would open her mouth and chew, but she never fully woke up. I would look at her face and sometimes kiss her; I would talk to her and tell her to wake up and take a shower, or say good night to my siblings, but she just slurred something under her breath that I couldn't understand. At the end of the night, while my brothers and sisters slept, I would be going through bags of hand-me-down clothes trying to find them outfits for the next day. Then I took a hot shower. I loved to let the water fall on my face; the hot water was so soothing, and for a second the anxiety stopped and I had a moment of calm to ask God to give me strength to face tomorrow.

It never failed -- tomorrow had its own hurtles to climb, and with each day it got harder and harder to survive. We often went without the bare necessities like deodorant and tissue. So over time we had to get creative and learn new innovative ways to cope. One of my mother's boyfriends taught me to rub soap under my arms after a shower as a substitute for deodorant, and we used newspaper in the place of tissue. Food often got low -- too low to manage -- so I would try to send my siblings to bed early, hoping they would forget about dinner and sleep through the night, but that rarely worked. One of them would always wake up complaining that they were hungry, so I had to take late-night walks with an old beat-up shopping cart to my great-grandmother's house for food. She lived across Crotona Park in the Bronx; we lived about fifteen blocks away. I was always terrified to leave the house so late, but I couldn't send them to bed hungry another night, and secretly I was starving just like they were. I'd run through that park as fast as I could, with the old shopping cart cracking and squeaking all the way there.

My great-grandmother would always give me the food I came for, but not before about an hour of listening to her talk about how my mother was so unfit, and how I had to make sure that I took care of those kids. I can still hear the weight of her voice. "You make sure those kids are clean, you understand me?" I would just sit in the little green chair by her dresser and nod my head. "Yes, Grandma," I would say with such confidence, to try to ease her worry as she would go on to explain, in detail, how to wash everybody from the baby to myself. It was drilled into my head, the burden of motherhood, and I had not even learned to ride a bike.

I soon realized I was a survivor, and it came naturally. I could cook, clean house, organize, and set a home atmosphere that I only wished I could experience myself.

I gave my siblings all of me. I dreamed of the day my mother could find the courage to give up drugs and become addicted to us, giving us all of her. I needed her to take her rightful place so I could one day relax, but I knew in my heart she would never be the mother of my dreams; it just wasn't her. I watched her strength come and go with each relationship. She had to have a man in her life. I couldn't understand why we weren't enough. Over time, I learned to respect her for who she was. She had so much love in her heart, all the good intentions in the world, but her life could never just revolve around us or herself alone. She needed love and intimacy that being a mother just couldn't fulfill.

When I was eleven years old, I woke up to what I thought was an ordinary morning. I dressed everybody for school and started my routine, which consisted of dropping off my sister Cherell at her classroom by 8:00 a.m., then André by 8:10; then I continued past my school up the hill to drop off George by 8:20. George was the second oldest under me, but he was born prematurely, with cerebral palsy, so he had to go to a special school. I had to be at school by 8:30, and as you can imagine, I was never on time. I can still hear Ms. Ramirez now; she made it her business to publicly address you when you came in late. I used to feel so humiliated stumbling into class, barely catching my breath from the tedious walk.

I never told her what was going on at home, but one day she asked me if I was interested in making a little money doing little odd jobs for her on the weekends. I was so grateful to her for that, because the extra twenty dollars could buy groceries for a week. I was taking care of things, or so I thought. By the end of that day, about 2 p.m., I got called to the office only to find Cherell and André sitting in the waiting area of the principal's office. I thought for sure they must have gotten in trouble, but just then a lady came up to us with a pen and a folder and told us we had to go with her and we would be coming back. I never made it back to C.E. S. 55 grammar school again. We picked up George next and we drove to the foster care agency. I wanted to throw up, I was so scared, but you would never know it. I looked calm and concerned, asking questions like a mother wanting to know what's going to happen to her children. I can still see their faces looking at me with a look that said, *What are we going to do, Shamina? Get us out of here.* We sat for hours trying to find a foster home that would be willing to take four kids. I couldn't stop thinking, *How did we get here?* My siblings were like vaults and you couldn't get them to tell you anything about our home life. We had discussed it before, and they knew better. Who would do this to us?

It was about 10:30 that night and we found what the system called a foster home in Queens. My baby sister, Tashi, was a newborn at the time; she was taken shortly after she was born and eventually given to her godmother, our aunt. The rest of us stayed in that foster home in Queens. I remember we pulled up to this old shaky-looking house, all of us clinging together at the arms in the back seat. I remember walking up the creaking steps to the front door, where we were greeted by a face I will never forget. I can't seem to remember her name, but her face I will never forget. She stood about five feet nine inches tall, and her skin was dark and discolored in some areas of her face. She wore thick, large-framed glasses that magnified her lazy eye on the right side. Her lips were large and dry as she slurred, "Y'all gonna sleep upstairs." Before I could even get a word out, the social worker turned and hurried out with an attitude. I guess because it took so long to find a placement for us, I believe that night she would have left us on a park bench if it meant getting home to her own family on time. As we walked up the stairs, the smells of dog and dirt hit you like a ton of bricks. At the top I noticed on the second floor there were only two bedrooms, and one belonged to the woman -- I could tell from the sloppy made-up larger bed, and the huge black Rottweiler that stood guard in front of the door.

The second room had two twin-size beds in it, and one was occupied by a little girl no older than nine years old. The woman looked at me and said, "The two girls can stay in here; the boys follow me. " I couldn't imagine where she was going to take them; there were no other rooms that I could see. She walked them to the end of the dark hallway, and I followed her every step of the way as she reached the end of the hall and began to walk up a tall, narrow staircase tucked away. Instantly my brothers began to scream and cry. I wanted to cry myself. I didn't know what was going on; it looked as if she was putting them in a dungeon. I shouted with everything in me, "Where are you taking them?"

She looked at me like a wild beast, her lazy eye dancing in her head, and said with spit flying from her mouth, "They got two beds in the attic! Now you ain't gonna come in here with no crazy shit! Boys sleep up in the attic and girls sleep downstairs!"

"They are little boys, not teenagers. They are not going up there alone!" I said. André was only about five years old and George was ten. I grabbed them close to me and held them tight. I thought I was going to have to fight this woman. She looked at me like she just knew I was some troubled kid and she would hurt me and think nothing of it if I made one wrong move. She threatened to call the cops on me, and I knew they would take her word for it and believe that I was another out-of-control foster kid. So I told her that I would walk them up there and put them to sleep. She became irate and ran to her room to call the cops.

By now my little sister Cherell was crying and screaming, "Just take them upstairs, Shamina, they're going to arrest you!" I couldn't even think straight. I had George and André clinging to my legs, screaming, Cherell screaming, this lady cursing and yelling, and I just wanted to break down, but I knew I couldn't. My siblings needed me, and I needed to know they were okay. Just as I was about to try to calm the situation down, I heard a bang at the door. It was the police. We all gathered downstairs, my siblings holding tightly to the banister and peeking from the top of the stairs. Just as I thought, the woman claimed I tried to hit her and encourage the other children to rebel against her. She told the cops how ungrateful foster kids are and how lucky I should feel.

I tried to express the truth and explain to the officers what really happened, but one of the officers yelled in a nasty, intimidating voice, "Shut up! Or I will haul you right out of here! I don't want to hear nothing you have to say!"

I felt hopeless and I just stood there as they talked about how my "druggy mama" abandoned us and how she could have us out on the street by morning. Eventually the cops left, but not without a warning. As they left, one officer leaned in toward me and said, "If we have to come back here tonight, you're spending the night in the juvenile detention center." With the little pride I had left, I walked up the stairs and met my siblings waiting at the top. I walked my sister to her room and told her to stay there, and then I took that long, dark walk up the stairs to the attic with my brothers. There were two twin beds side by side, separated by an old nightstand with a broken top drawer, and on top there was a lamp with no shade. I quickly turned on the lamp and laid them both down on their beds. I remember the look in their blood-red eyes from screaming and crying as I told them to rest, that I was going to leave the light on and that I was right downstairs watching everything and I wasn't going to let anybody come up here and hurt them. I sat there and rubbed their backs till their tired red eyes closed.

I left the door open and softly walked down the dark steps. I got halfway down and my legs just collapsed, and I sat on the step and cried, with my hand over my mouth to muffle the sound. I was terrified and exhausted. By the time I got back to my room, my sister was sleeping. She had befriended the little girl who was there, and that made it easier for her.

The next week a new social worker came to visit, and I told her everything. I told her we had to get out of there. I thank God for her sincerity, and she worked quickly to find us a new placement. A few days later we received word that we were scheduled to leave in a week. We didn't move to a new foster home, but rather they attempted to place us with family members. It was during that time that I heard rumors of who called social services on us. I heard it was my mother's aunt, who called after discovering my mother was still using drugs during her pregnancy with my little sister, but I don't know how true that is. For all we know it could have been the next-door neighbor, who would help us out from time to time. I guess I'll never know for sure. What I do know is that things just seemed to keep getting worse. Being placed with family members didn't work out as smooth as they thought – even our family wanted to get paid, and social services never sent the checks on time, so we all had to be split up in the end—some with family and some in a foster home. My heart fell to my stomach. I couldn't shake this constant nausea. *Are they okay? Are they scared? Where is my mother? What did she do when we never came home?* These questions consumed my thoughts. I had let them down.

A year had passed and my mother successfully managed to complete her rehabilitation program. I was so reluctant to get excited, fearing she would relapse, but I couldn't help the feeling of joy. We were reuniting and we would finally be together again. Everybody was so different. We were split up between Hempstead, New York; Edison, New Jersey; and the heart of the Bronx. I worried about how the relationship between my siblings and me would be after so much time apart. I feared my siblings might blame me for what happened, but to my surprise it made us tighter than ever. My mom was sober now, and while she was in the rehabilitation program -- no surprise -- she met a man who became our permanent house guest since the first night we all spent together. I was so happy to see my siblings again and to look at their faces. I was so happy that I didn't even have time to argue with my mother about inviting a strange man to live with us so soon, after all we had gone through. I was just grateful to be together again. I missed my sister so much -- we had shared a room for so long, and when I looked beside me and didn't see her there, it was the hardest thing to deal with. Even as a little girl, her very presence gave me strength. It was something in her that helped me cope -- and she didn't even have to speak. She was more than a sister; she was the only friend I had who understood what I was dealing with.

Our first day home we all just looked at each other, so nervous, not knowing what to say to each other. I remember gazing at my sister in awe. I wondered if things could be the way they used to be between us. After a few hours of the awkward silence, I decided to start a conversation about anything just to let them know that I was still the same old Shamina. Later on that day I brushed her hair, which had grown down her back, and we just played. The innocence of laughing together again, imagining and dreaming together under the same roof was the most soothing feeling in the world, and things seemed to fall back into place. During my eighth-grade year in school, we moved to Jersey City, New Jersey in hopes of escaping the Bronx and making a fresh start.

With my mother sober and fairly happy in her new relationship, she did her best to be the best mom she could be. This meant I had a little time to focus on me, and I was not happy with what I saw. I hated my body. The stress and strain had left their mark, which seemed to hang over my face like a dark veil I couldn't seem to remove. I was determined to change it before high school, so I pushed myself to dangerous limits, drinking Slim-Fast shakes, skipping meals, working out till I passed out, running track, and diet pills—I tried it all. I pushed and pushed, determined not to be swallowed up by my reality, like a forty-year-old woman fighting to get her groove back. I was so hard on myself. I lost the weight, and I was ready for Ferris High School…or so I thought.

It would be during the next four years that I would discover I wasn't invincible. I had a weakness, and it was love. It was like a drug to me. I thirsted for the opportunity of its closeness; the suspense and the thrill of it set my soul in flight. I became consumed with my daydreams of love -- finally I found something that made me feel like I could escape into a world where I could convince myself I was receiving just as much as I was putting out. I was free, if only for a season.

CHAPTER 4

Pandora's Box

I always seemed to attract men who were older than me, but none of them ever thought enough of me to openly claim me as their girlfriend. I was always "cool peoples" or "a special friend" and in some cases just another groupie, all so far from the person I really was. I was joy, I was life, I was vibrant, and I was whole, once upon a time, but life has a funny way of changing a person. I opened Pandora's Box, and one after another, lovers giving and then taking, nothing came free. I paid for it all with my innocence till I had nothing left.

DURING MY TEENAGE years I met a few men whom I cared for or became infatuated with, but they never truly had a piece of my heart. My journey with love began the day my mother came home with the phone number of a producer she had met at the bank. She happened to notice he was wearing a jacket from a very popular record company, and she approached him, telling him he had to help her daughter, who wanted to become an R&B singer. He gave my mother a number and she gave it to me to call. I was so excited and nervous at the same time; back then I think everybody wanted to be a rapper, singer, or poet—it was all about the arts. After a few days of doubting myself, I finally got the guts to call the number.

Mr. Producer and I talked briefly during our first call and scheduled a time to meet in person. I was fifteen years old at the time and all I could think about was music, so it seemed like a dream come true. The evening that he showed up to my house, I was surprised to see that he was so young. I was expecting some older guy to walk through the door, but he was in his early twenties and had been producing music for some time. My mother knew how bad I wanted to become an artist, so she allowed me to break a lot of the rules that she normally would enforce. I was able to go with Mr. Producer freely, and it became normal to spend long hour's together and late nights.

When I think back, I still don't know how things changed from business to pleasure, but I never made it to any studios, nor did we ever really talk about my career at all. He would pick me up and we would drive around to some of the nearby churches he played keyboard for. He was also a musician. On one occasion we went to a hotel, just to be close with each other and talk. I was still a virgin at the time, and he never forced me to rush into anything sexual. Our relationship stayed like that for two whole years. I guess that's one of the reasons I fell in love with him. I've experienced other relationships before, but it was nothing more than puppy love. Most of the time guys would conveniently lose my number when they found out I was a virgin, but Mr. Producer was different. He was a Christian, and although he worked for a major record company, he was well known for using his instrumental talents in the church. He was also gentle and had a passion for the arts that I could relate to. He was far from perfect and I had my suspicions that he was entertaining other women. At the time he had a female "best friend" that I was concerned about, but I never complained because I had no reason to believe that he would ever mislead me like that. It wasn't easy keeping that trust alive, especially when I was hearing all kinds of rumors about him being married. Though he claimed to be separated when I asked him about it, I still had my doubts, but I wanted to believe he cared.

It was August when life as I knew it changed forever. My mother got married that month and left me alone for a week while she went on her honeymoon. That week I broke my virginity with Mr. Producer. I had no idea what I was doing, but I was in love. My mother had been gone for two days, and I invited him over to the house. I remember telling him over the phone how ready I was to take things to the next level. When I hung up I couldn't believe what I had said. The whole house seemed quiet. Everybody was asleep. My heart was racing, waiting for him to get there. Finally I heard his car door slam and a knock on the door. When he walked in, I felt like running out, I was so scared. We sat in the living room and I remember having a sheet draped over my lap, sitting on the coach watching TV. He sat next to me and I could feel the palms of my hands beginning to sweat. I went numb as I felt his hand move slowly under the sheet and up my nightgown. After about ten minutes I got up and went into the kitchen and he followed. Pressing his body against mine from behind me, he was ready for something I had never known, but I was willing to pretend. So I suggested we go upstairs to my room. I felt like my legs were going to collapse with each step up the stairs. I still remember the touch that made me feel grown, how I floated away on the simplicity of a lover's caress. I laid on the bed with my heart beating out of my chest. He asked me if I had a condom and of course I didn't so, naïve, I laid back without a care in the world, trusting that he knew what he was doing. As we began to have sex, it was uncomfortable to say the least. I don't know whether it was the slight pain or that this moment seemed a lot more loving and passionate in my dreams.

Whatever it was, I was turned off, the mood shifted, and it lost its spark. I instantly started to feel so dumb. I had no idea that I deserved more than that. I was so ashamed, but it didn't last long. After a few minutes he stopped and his exact words were "Let me stop. I don't want to get you in any trouble. "I was kind of glad because I couldn't describe what I felt, but it wasn't what I thought it would be like. I was embarrassed and confused. So many thoughts ran through my head at once. And to make matters worse, the next day he was scheduled to go out of town for a few days on business. He called me every day to see how I was feeling, and that made me feel a lot better, but I couldn't help feeling like I disappointed him or I failed to satisfy him. My mind began to play tricks on me. I can remember asking myself, *What does he want with an inexperienced girl like me?* I had just turned seventeen; I knew he probably had someone else that I didn't know anything about.

My thoughts got so bad that I told my mother what I had

done when she got back. She was not surprised to find out we had feelings for each other; she simply stated that she was disappointed in him. She had so much respect for him, and she always thought he would wait until I was of age to handle something like this. I remember the night she invited him over to talk openly about what happened. When he was asked about our sexual encounter, he sat right in front of me and said, "Like many of the young girls I work with, I take them around a lot of stars and sometimes they develop feelings for me…"

My mouth dropped. Instantly I asked myself, *Is he saying what I think he's saying?* He sat there and denied ever touching me. He blew me off as if I was some young groupie; star struck from all the glitz and glamour of the music industry. I sat across from him, looking straight into his eyes as I cried. I couldn't believe what I was hearing, and the part that hurt the most was he seemed so unaffected by my tears. For months after, I placed myself in a box, never leaving the porch of my house. I would sit there for hours watching the cars go by. Occasionally I would see him driving by my house, looking at me through his passenger side window as he passed. I couldn't stop thinking about what he said to me when he first found out that I was a virgin. He said, "Do you know how special that is in God's sight? I don't want to be the one to open that door for you." It wasn't until after this experience that I truly understood what he meant by opening a door you can't close. He was right, a door had been opened and I was never going to be the same. From that moment I knew I would never love the same. I had become a woman and I didn't know the magnitude of what came along with that territory, but life taught me quickly.

Months had passed and I still couldn't get over what he said sitting there on my mother's couch. I was haunted by the rumors he spread of how I lied about everything. He told everybody—friends of mine who knew him got an earful of how I was a lying, delusional girl and he had no idea why I would do something like this to him. His words haunted me. I mean, I was a child who went to school with holes in her shoes, my bras tied in knots under my arms just to keep them up, and yet I had never been made to feel as humiliated as I did that day. I vowed never to let anyone devalue me like that again. As a result I became overly consumed with how I was perceived, and my low self-esteem often got the best of me. I hid the real me behind a hard shell I had created for my own protection, but that shield didn't stand a chance against what was coming my way.

I was seventeen and a junior in high school, and I could count the friends that I made on one hand. After such a rocky start to womanhood, in high school I never really gave people the opportunity to get to know me. I always used the excuse that everybody was so immature and I was just too mature to find something in common with them. Ironically the few girlfriends I did make during high school were just like me; they dated guys who had graduated already, between twenty and twenty-four years old. We all had the same heir about us, but they still seemed to be so free unlike me, I was always so cautious after what I went through with Mr. Producer. This obsession with the opinions of others caused me to isolate myself from everybody, in fear of being rejected or misunderstood. I vowed to never feel the way I did that day, but in spite of the hurt I sometimes felt and the depression I so often fell into, I never stopped believing in love. I had such a desire to fall in love, to escape with someone who could see past all the smoke and ashes straight into my heart. I saw visions of myself finally free, happy in love, starting a family, and finally showing my family how it's done; but being only seventeen years old I had a lot more lessons to learn. Besides, the guys my age were just looking for a good time, and after all I'd been through, that was the one thing I found hard to do.

One afternoon during recess, my close friend and I sat outside. It was May and the sun was showering over us. It was one of those days you just knew something was bound to happen. We sat in our regular spots, far enough from the little cliques that Ferris High School was known for, but close enough to get a good look at somebody who could become our afternoon laugh. Then it happened. I saw him walking back from lunch, smiling and full of life. He seemed so confident, in his own world.

To this day I still don't know whether to thank God or curse the devil for ever having seen him, but I did. He was like no other boy I'd ever seen before. He was well groomed and, boy, could he dress, unlike all the other boys with their fitted caps and jerseys all seeming to mesh together, unable to tell one from another. He wore blazers, applejack hats, and French cuff shirts. I remember thinking he looked like he jumped out of a neo-soul magazine. I was so intrigued by his sophistication. Something in me shifted and I knew I had to get to know him, but I was a lady, and I was so old-fashioned I could have never approached him, not even for his friendship—it just wasn't my style. I tapped my friend and said with such innocence and sincerity, "Who is that?" She responded by saying, "Who, E? You know he's gay, right?" And my naive self replied, "Well, you can tell there's more to him, like he lives a real life outside of this high school, and I want to know his story." Those words left my lips with such confidence, as if I had some sort of knowledge about what it meant to be gay or to know someone who was. I felt a pulling and overwhelming feeling that I had to get to know him. It was purely innocent at the time; I had no romantic expectation for E. I guess that's why my feelings were unlike anything I had ever experienced in my life. I had to talk to him; I had to know his secrets, who he was behind all the smiles and laughs. I knew to look behind the mask that I too knew so well.

I can still remember the first time he caught my attention. We shared a class together and he found me sitting in the back of the room dressed in my usual black or brown, hiding behind my straight brown hair. He sat at the table closest to mine with a few of his other friends; they'd tell jokes like they often did, but that day was different. I felt like he was trying to get my attention and he did it; he said something that tickled me from the inside out. As I think back on that day, I still can't remember the joke, but I sure do remember the laugh I bellowed out from my nearby table. In that moment I felt something happen; a connection was made that was electrifying. We laughed till we had tears in our eyes, and as the laughter subsided, we managed to catch each other's eye, and I will never forget the look he gave me. It was like he was so happy that I was smiling, and smiling at him. He had a sense of accomplishment on his face as if he had succeeded in what he set out to do.

The class was over shortly, and during lunch a mutual friend introduced us. We spent the rest of the year as friends from a distance. It was weird—he would always say hi to me when he saw me in the hallways, and when we hung out during lunch from time to time, he would always say that I was his wife and that we were going to get married. I always thought it was a joke. I could have never guessed it would end up that way. It was much easier to forget my feelings for Mr. Producer when E was around, even if we only saw each other in school; he gave me something else to think about.

E disappeared during junior year. I heard he moved out of state, and once again I was forced back into reality. It was when E left that things seemed so much harder to handle, but I decided to atempt to have a normal life that didnt involve constent sorrow. I got over Mr. Producer and I finally decided to step off that front porch and start living again, and I walked right into the arms of a young man I like to call Truth. Now he, too, produced music and loved the arts. He was driven not by love or relationship, but by business. He is perhaps the most driven man I know, and I knew I could lean on him because he could handle it. We stimulated each other's minds, and he is the only man I have ever met who could have a debate with me and leave me speechless by the end. He never rolled over and let me win. He was not intimidated at all by my mature, critical, motherly demeanor. I had to be ready for a challenge when it came to him, and I loved him for that. He forced me out of my own way, and I had no choice but to see things differently. Long before any thoughts of a romantic relationship crossed my mind, we were best friends. He would come and pick me up from my house on days that my mother and I would have some of our awful fights. I found refuge with him. I would call him during all hours of the night after I had one of my regular nightmares, as I so often had, and he would listen and we would fall asleep on the phone together. We talked about everything; there were very few decisions made in both of our lives that we didn't equally make. We did everything together. I was like his little sidekick, and whenever you saw him, you saw me. All his friends thought something was going on between us, and he loved keeping everybody in suspense, guessing.

I dated a friend of his for a few months until I discovered he had a live-in girlfriend who was about seven months pregnant, but Truth was right there to cushion my fall. We often did that for one another. I remember the night everything changed. We sat in his room in the dark with one candle lit and we just talked, as we always did. He reached in surprisingly to hold me closer to him, and I knew that this feeling was unlike any we had shared before. It was sweet and passionate, but I pulled away, fearful of what might happen if his friend found out that we were getting too close. I knew we weren't together anymore, but I never wanted to be labeled a whore. I can still see the way he looked at me when I told him that. His expression said it all, he looked as if he knew all to well his friend's reputation of being a dog and he didn't want me to worry about that. I surrendered in his arms and buried my head in his chest. I took a deep breath of his cologne. The smell of his body covered every part of me; I became him, exchanging my worries for his strength. He was very masculine and his arrogance intrigued me. He was never a very passionate or deep man in the sense of emotions, but I like to believe I brought a sense of depth into his life that was not there before. He was so sure of himself that it allowed me—no, it *forced* me to relax. We laid there with innocence in the atmosphere; both of us had never embarked on such intimacy. We began exchanging simple, subtle, yet sensual touches until we couldn't take it anymore, and that was the night two friends became lovers. I was so afraid. I didn't want to lose a friend. I had fought myself so hard to allow our friendship to become what it was. I trusted him and grew a dependency for his company, his point of views, and I could only hope that I wasn't making a mistake.

After that night there were many more to come; we had a wild attraction to each other, and I felt comfortable and stable. I was still very inexperienced, but he was a good teacher and I learned quickly how to satisfy him. I found myself wanting more of his love. I remember the first time I got up the nerve to tell him I loved him, and his response—a thank you. Needless to say that was when things started to change, and I noticed that after we had shared countless intimate nights, days, and evenings together, he was still involved with other women. Unlike me, he was able to keep us in the friend zone. He spoke to me about his other relationships as they began to notice the change in him, how he never came around anymore and hardly called. I couldn't help but to fall into place and give my advice or point of view; besides, we were friends to begin with, and I never did discuss what was to come after our first encounter, so we sort of just stayed in limbo when it came to making a commitment and becoming monogamous.

I remember a discussion we had about a girl he was

dating. He said she cheated on him, and I said to him, "Aren't you cheating on her?" He looked at me and said, "No, you were here before her, and you'll be here after her," as if I was an exception to the rule. I didn't know just how true his statement was at the time, but after years and countless attempts to win his heart and his commitment, nothing worked. Whenever I brought up our relationship, he came up with some reason why we shouldn't complicate things with superficial titles. He said people change when you start using labels. I began to feel unappreciated and used. The exclusive friendship he had created for me was not enough, and it played on my self-esteem. I began to wonder, what he was so afraid of losing by being in a committed relationship. I couldn't help but to think maybe I wasn't so special after all. I questioned how many others there were who believed they were special. Suddenly the arrogant attitude that once turned me on just made me sick. His lack of empathy and sensitivity just infuriated me and I wondered how a person could be so self absorbed. If it wasn't about money, business or sex I rarely got a straight answer from him. We started arguing constantly and he stopped calling as much and I started calling more. Towards the end, the arguments got so bad and I became obsessed with my mission to get him to understand how he was making me feel. I tried to leave, but our bodies would always draw us back to each other regardless of how angry we were. For two people who weren't in a relationship, it was sure felt like one.

Then, the possibility of ever having a normal relationship fell apart one afternoon. I was walking home from a nearby friend's house when it began to rain, so I stopped by his house to get an umbrella. When I walked in, it was a very different feeling I got from everybody. I was like family. I called his mother "Mom" and walked freely through her house; I felt I had gained her trust and love. But that day was different, and everybody seemed so tense and uncomfortable. I walked into the living room, where his sister greeted me as usual. I happened to glance down and notice a beautiful baby girl sitting in a bouncing seat; she had a beautiful chocolate brown complexion and a head full of hair. I asked his sister, "Whose baby is this?" And I received the answer that flipped my world upside down. She said, "This is Truth's baby. You didn't know?" I began to boil inside like lava waiting to erupt. I got so dizzy, but I kept a good face and replied, "You're kidding. I had no idea, he never told me." She took the baby and left the room. I sat there for a minute waiting to see if he was going to come downstairs. I knew she had to have told him I was here, and that I knew what was going on.

After a few minutes of sitting in the room alone, I got up and began to walk up the stairs to his room. The game was on and he had friends over; I thought to myself this scene could not have gone any worse. I walked in the room full of cheering men and looked around and he was not there. I looked in the room next door to it and he was standing inside with his daughter in his arms. I could tell his sister got to him two seconds before me, by the look on his face. I couldn't muster up the words to say, so I looked him in his eyes with tears falling down my face and said, "You liar." I turned away and fumbled down the stairs. My knees were so weak and my legs felt like sand bags. After passing his daughter off to his sister, he tried to stop me, but I just cried as we tussled for the door. He tried to kiss me, but I turned away. The kiss that I once believed could heal everything now seemed like a desperate attempt to cloud my focus.

I finally broke free and with my heart in my hand I walked what seemed like forever that night, with the rain pouring down my face and my body bent over toward the ground. My stomach was in a knot. I struggled to stand up straight because of the pain. I cried so hard that night as I walked through the park by his house. I remember the rain pounding on my head; I could barely see in front of me. I yelled at the top of my lungs, "God, why won't you just take me now! Why does it always have to end like this?" But God never answered me that night.

By the time I got home, I was drenched, and weary. I was back at square one again. It was hard to hide the pain I felt, so I didn't; I walked around the house like a zombie, crying off and on, so detached from reality.

After about a week, Truth tried to go back to the way it was before, but with a newborn baby to attend to, it only made it more obvious how much things had changed. He tried to allow me to do what I had to in order to get over the situation; he even listened as I ranted and raved about how hurt I was and how awful he was for doing this to me. He listened until he just couldn't take it anymore, and I was so bitter I just couldn't stop. I guess it made it easy after a while for him to cut me out of the picture. I was so confused. I wanted to be there with him and the baby somehow, but I just couldn't shake the bitter taste in my mouth when I thought about another woman carrying his child; it felt like a piece of me was dying. What hurt most of all is that I had no idea it was happening right under my nose. I had so much respect for him, so much trust in him that I really didn't know if I could ever see him again. We shared a few nights together after that, but it had lost its sting. And just when I thought I was going to go off the deep end, out of nowhere E shows up just in time to save me.

It was the end of my senior year. He came back in time to take me to the prom and to save me from self-destruction. I had asked Truth to take me, but he declined of course. Things were so different between us. I wasn't surprised, but I have no regrets. E made sure I had the time of my life. It was one of the best days of my life, and I was floating on a cloud. I had my best friend with me, and he brought me joy. That night I was crowned prom queen, and I was on top of the world. I can still hear the host call my name, and immediately following, I heard E's voice yelling and cheering from on top of the banquet table. I wanted the night to last forever or at least all night. I was a good girl, so my mother granted permission on prom night to stay out all night, and to this day I think it was a trick gift because I had nowhere to stay and nothing to do all night. I remember telling E that I had the chance to stay out all night and that's exactly what I wanted to do. I told him I didn't care if we had to spend the night on a park bench; there was no way I was going home. So I suggested we go to a hotel and stay the night.

That night I noticed something weird about E. The way he looked at me gave me chills. It was unlike anything I had ever seen from him; it was intense. Afraid of the unknown, I asked a girlfriend of mine to play third wheel and spend the night with us at the hotel. There was only one problem; I didn't have any reservations booked, and my naive self had no idea that it would be so hard on prom night to get a hotel. Our limo driver drove us around for an hour, trying to find an available room. We ended up having to stay at a motel on the highway that we were pretty sure belonged to the local prostitutes in the area. It was horrible, but we laughed all night. My girlfriend just fell asleep, and it was like she wasn't even there. I can still remember at about 4 a.m. running across the highway in our prom clothes to a small burger spot. The whole time we laughed so hard we almost wet our pants. It was so imperfect and yet so just right for me.

After prom he disappeared again. I never knew why at such a young age he never could stay in one place for too long. But I always kept an eye out for his return. I knew he would come back to me. He always did.

CHAPTER **5**

Out on My Own

AFTER GRADUATION I got my first job at a bank. I was nineteen years old, and the first thing I did was get my own place. It was time for me to go out into the world on my own. Leaving my mother's house was like lifting a weight off my shoulders. I could finally create my own place of peace. I moved from a small, cramped room full of sorrow and despair to a one-bedroom apartment in one of the worst neighborhoods in Jersey City, but I didn't care—it was mine and I was finally home. Everything seemed to be going great.

I was still messing around with Truth from time to time, but we could never find that fit we once had. It was like trying to play with your favorite toy after it's broken. You find yourself so committed to what seems routinely comfortable, but you never really enjoy it like you used to. I always kept my eyes open for the day that I would bump into E again. I had my own place now, so we could stay up and laugh and talk all night if we wanted to. I needed his energy, some sort of comic relief from my reality, and that is exactly what I got, and more.

It was my first summer in my apartment. I was coming home from work, and to my surprise, I bumped into E right on my block. It was just as I thought it would be; he came upstairs for dinner and we laughed and talked the whole night. I told him about Truth and how he broke my heart, and you would have thought it happened to him. He was so hurt for me, and that was new to me. I'd never had someone show such empathy for what I was going through.

We stayed together so often that you would have thought we lived together. He hated the drama between me and Truth, and frankly Truth never really trusted E. I tried to tell him that he was just my friend, but he never fully believed that, and neither did I. There was always something deeper, some unspoken understanding or binding of our two worlds, that at times seemed eerie. As inseparable as we became, I knew that E was holding back something from me. He always seemed like a vault full of secrets, and I was determined to know who he really was—why he sometimes seemed so happy, but at other times he seemed so distant. It was no surprise that E was never able to stay put long enough for me to dig as deep into him as I wanted to. He disappeared again and all I could do was wait until fate brought us back around again.

About a year had past and our paths crossed again. This time it was a miracle I was able to recognize him because he looked nothing like the E I remembered. He was wearing a mini jean skirt with a tank top, gold hoop earrings, a pair of stiletto sandals that strapped around the ankle, a matching purse clutched under his arm and a long ponytail that fell to the middle of his back. My initial reaction was one of excitement. I was so ecstatic to see him again that without thinking I yelled from my car window, "E, wait right there!" He looked startled, but he stopped. Later on that day we laughed about it over drinks at my house. I had no idea that I had completely outed him in broad daylight, but he got over it.

As we sat in my house that day, everything in me wanted to ask him what the hell was going on. But I didn't want him to feel judged. He was back in my life, and I knew we would eventually get to the bottom of it. I waited about a week and I brought up the issue of him cross-dressing. He told me it was just for making money, and he had no other way to support himself right now. I still had so many questions, and I just couldn't hold my tongue. I came right out and asked him if he was out there whoring; we both chuckled for a second because it was such an outrageous question—a question that you would never think you would find yourself asking a man. Yet after the laughs subsided, I was really hoping that wasn't the case. He told me that he never slept with anybody; he was just a dancer at a gentlemen's club. Instantly I said to him, "They don't know you're a man?" He found my naïve demeanor to be so amusing, but I was so concerned. He told me that no one knew he was a man; he was very good at what he did and he was never sloppy. I couldn't imagine how risky and dangerous that could be, but I knew what it was like to have to go to someone and beg for money or food because you have no other way, so I felt empathy for him and it made us even closer. He would sometimes leave from my house to go to work at night. One day I sat in the bathroom with him and watched him make up his face; I was so facinated, it was nothing like anything I had ever seen, but I was always worried for him. I got a chance to know parts of E I had never known before; I was getting to know the real him, and I was surprised at what I discovered. E was raised for the most part by his grandmother, and he was raised in church. He sang in the choir, and his grandmother was the first lady, her husband the pastor of their own Christian church. I couldn't believe he came from such a spiritually rooted foundation.

I, on the other hand, had no idea what it was like to have such a background. I always loved God, and before E came back into my life, I was attending Sunday service at a small Baptist church with no more than ten members, but I didn't grow up in a home where it was normal to go to church or even pray regularly. E took me by the hand and introduced me to a whole new world. I can remember the first time he took me to church with him. His family had closed down their church and sold the building some years ago, so we went to a night service at a church his grandmother attended.

I was speechless when I pulled up to his house. His hair and beard were cut with precision. He wore a tailored suit and tie, and he had on very expensive shoes and a Bible in his hand. I almost drove past him because I didn't recognize him. He got into the car, and his cologne filled the space. I was taken by the way he moved differently; it was like a new man. His voice was so deep; I was startled when he said, "What's up?" We went back to my house before service began, and he worked his magic on me. He did my hair, makeup, and picked out my clothes for me. I felt so uncomfortable—I felt I was overdressed for church, but E assured me I was okay, and I hoped he was right. It was my first time in heels, and I was so nervous.

That night I was introduced to the Pentecostal denomination. When I got there I knew I was home; the spirit was so high in that church. They sang songs and worshiped God for hours, and it was the most expressive thing I had ever seen. After that night he rarely let me see him in women's clothing, and I found myself anticipating when I was going to get the chance to see the side of him that I saw that night at his grandmother's church. I was thirsty to know more about him and about church.

I couldn't stop thing about the women I saw there, all dressed so beautifully in their suits and matching hat. Some of them were loud and outspoken, and some were a bit quiet and meek and some could sing like angels. The one thing I will never forget was the glow. It was a calming glow that seemed to hang over the faces of some of the women, too many to be a coincidence. It was inviting and it looked like they were so happy and at peace. What fueled these women? Where did their passion come from? I needed to know, and E was willing to show me what he thought being a woman of God was. He taught me how to dress, how to do my makeup, and how to carry myself in the house of God, but sometimes I felt like he was a little too hard on me. At times it felt like it was a little too much, and I wondered if he was taking me further away from that glow I sought to find. I wondered if everybody had to go through this much trouble just to get ready to go worship God, but I always wanted to be portrayed as an honorable woman, and I figured E knew better than me, some poor young girl from the projects, so I followed his instructions, and there was no telling where they would lead me.

CHAPTER **6**

A Man That Findeth a Wife...

I WAS TWENTY-THREE years old when E and I decided to be in an exclusive relationship. It happened one night during one of our long conversation about our hopes and dreams. That night I told E my fears and he told me his. We agreed never to leave each others side no matter what this life would take us through. It was then that E said he was ready to be in a relationship. I still remember the sound of E's voice when I told him I was afraid of him, afraid of how he could break my heart because of his past. He was a little hurt that I could ever be afraid of him. He told me that he knew what he wanted for his life, and that spending the rest of his life with a man living a homosexual lifestyle was not his hearts desire. He expressed how much he wanted children and a wife, how he never loved a woman the way he loved me and he couldn't see his life without me in it. I was overcome with emotion and love. I had no choice but to believe him, after all he had been the most consistent person in mylife, so I trusted him. I just kept thinking about the way he accepted me just as I was, given the fact that I was no polished or refined girl, I had nothing to offer him but my heart and alot of scars to heal, yet somehow that was enough for him. I felt such a sense of obligation to accept him despite his past, the way he embraced me, in spite of mine. I agreed to see just how far we could go in a romantic relationship. Now, I'm not going to lie to you, I was afraid, —Afraid of what might happen if this ended badly. I often stopped myself from thinking about just how bad things could get, and I focused on the miraculous testimony we would have if we could manage to put the past behind us and truly move forward with our relationship. At first my intentions were to take things slow, but that didn't exist in our world. When we got together everything happened fast. As a whole we had little patience when it came down to getting what we wanted; we were in love and there was no stopping us. We moved together like two race cars speeding down our own highway— the possibilities were endless and we weren't afraid to crash. I wasn't surprised when less than a few months later E was talking marriage.

I never got the fairy-tale proposal I expected from E, no down on one knee tear-jerker. It was more like I walked right into it. Late one night we went for a ride around Country Village in Jersey City— it was E's idea. I had never been to this area, but it was beautiful. The houses had white picket fences, neatly cut bushes on the lawn, and the streets were so quiet and clean. It was like something out of a movie, and I loved it. These were the kind of houses I always saw myself starting a family of my own in. Afterwards, we parked the car in front of his grandmother's house and we sat and talked. E asked me, "If I asked you to marry me, what would you say?" and without a second thought said, "Yes; I would probably say yes." Instantly I thought to myself, *What do I have to lose? I've been hurt by strangers and hurt by friends alike, and meeting E has been the most real and intimate relationship I have ever experienced.* He picked up the phone and called his sister right after I said yes and he said to her, "I'm getting married."

After about three months of bliss, our scheduled date of July 16, 2005 was canceled over some blown-out-of-proportion argument we so often had. He left about four months before the wedding —leaving me with angry bridesmaids, a lot of money wasted, and a bunch of "I told you so's". I can still remember the day he left. I got home from work to find the house completely trashed. Curtains ripped down, everything was torn apart or knocked over, and I noticed he destroyed a wedding book I was making for memories and left it in the middle of a pile of garbage.

July 16th came and went; needless to say it was one of the saddest and longest days of my life —I slept the whole day away. A few weeks later E's grandmother passed away. I knew his world was in a state of chaos; she was the only person besides myself that E could depend on. I remember rushing to his side, forgetting all that we had gone through just weeks ago. I found him sitting in his grandmother's apartment crying his eyes out. I knew I wasn't going to leave him that way, so I stayed. I was prepared to move in and be there for him, no matter how long it took. A week after the funeral, E became obsessed with us setting another wedding date. I wanted us to take our time and do things right without all the rush. That was the last thing E wanted to hear. He was so bothered by the fact that I wasn't jumping out of my skin to marry him. During one of our conversations, he gave me what I believe was the worst proposal a woman could ever get. He said to me, "I'm going to get married with or without you, so you better get on board; it's happening and I just wanted to give you the first opportunity." I'm not sure whether I was feeding off his energy or perhaps I was in fact scared of him finding someone else, but I felt a sudden urgency to just give in. I knew that he needed something to cling to now that his grandmother was gone. I knew I was the best thing for him. I feared what he might run into out there. I didn't want him to crash and have a meltdown, so I volunteered to be a personal shield, trying to protect him from the inevitable—life.

I didn't care anymore about his past, for the possibility of his future with me seemed greater than it all. I saw his struggles and his issues, as unusual circumstances that I was fully capable of nurturing and loving away. There was such a feeling in me when it came to E, despite the evident warning signs, I felt like I had to do it. Something in me just kept feeling like if I didn't take this leap with him, he would go so crazy that he would kill himself.

Many say that I am crazy for taking such a chance on a man with so many issues and I can't say I blame them; yet at the time, I needed to be everything he needed. I found myself in a position I had occupied so often —the protector, and the caregiver sacrificing to make someone else happy. Although I loved him, I knew we were rushing things.

Telling my family was a disaster. They had loved E so long, as he was a friend who helped me laugh more and dressed me up like a doll, but, he was no husband that any mother would be glad to give her daughter to. So they fought us tooth and nail, but that just drew us closer into each other; it was us against the world and we raced forward.

On August 26, 2005, we got married secretly at the justice of the peace. We figured since no one approved, we should just go on with it alone but we weren't satisfied; this was not our hearts' desire. We had a vision of a beautiful ceremony and a reception surrounded by our family and friends. Unhappy with our decision, we began planning our wedding. It was so hard to plan a wedding without my sister or mother present. We struggled to pay for it all ourselves. Nobody wanted to have anything to do with it. I remember having to go with E to get my dress fitted, and he was as supportive as he could be, but it was nothing like being surrounded by your mother and smiling bridesmaids.

We had balances owed up until the hour of the wedding. I was so grateful for the monetary gifts we did receive. I didn't get my wedding dress until a week before the wedding. I worked something out with the dress shop, and they agreed to give me the dress despite my balance owed. E had his suit tailor made, and I still don't know how he got his suit the night before the wedding. We had no more money and no way to pay the balance he owed, and to this day I'm still afraid to ask.

On October 29, 2005 we pulled off a wedding ceremony and a full five-hour reception in only three months. As I think back on that experience, it was the only thing we had ever accomplished as a couple working together. The day of the wedding was a true reflection of our relationship; it was complete chaos for me. The maid of honor showed up without her hair done, I had to argue with my mother, and everybody was in slow motion. We didn't get to the church until 7 p.m., the time the reception was supposed to start. I was so upset with the lack of respect for the money, time, and energy that it took to plan this wedding. I wasted most of my time telling people off and waiting for my maid of honor to get her hair done.

Once the ceremony began, it was beautiful and it went exactly as planned. The reception, on the other hand, was a flop. The DJ I hired decided to hire someone else who had no clue what I was trying to do. We never got to dance our first dance, the DJ couldn't get our song right, and he played the up-tempo gospel song we had planned to use for the wedding party dance. We never received the top part of our cake because we had too many guests who invited themselves, and we didn't have enough cake to serve them, so we had to use the anniversary top cake to serve everybody. I was so exhausted that I just wanted it to be over.

At the end of the night, things just got worse. We had to take people home and then we finally got to our hotel room. It was small, but it was beautiful and cozy with a great view of the city, and we just took a minute to digest all that had happened. E seemed to be so proud of me; he was so happy. The way he looked at me made me feel so beautiful. That night, at that moment everything was perfect.

You Are My Friend

After we got married I couldn't believe my life, it was so amazing. I would come home to bubble baths filled with rose petals and he would just sit in the bathroom with me and talk. I felt like finally I was living, laughing and loving harder than I ever thought possible. I married my best friend and whenever we where together nothing else mattered. I was finally starting to love the woman I saw looking back at me in the mirror. E had such a gift for interpreting everything I wanted to be, everything I wanted to convey to the world and manifesting it into a unique style that I couldn't get enough of. E had an agenda and his first call to order was to party! And that we did. The party would start in the house as we were getting dressed and he would bring home a bottle of some fancy champagne and pour me a glass as I took my bath. I remember hating the bitter taste, but I would always take slow sips as if to say I was no stranger to the finer things, and then there was the music, it felt just like when I was younger and my farther would have the house ringing with music; E was the same way. I can recall very few moments that we shared that didn't have a song attached to it. He would walk around the house singing and dancing and in my mind I couldn't imagine the night getting any better, but it always did.

We would head to New York or our favorite bar and just find a quiet table in the back to relax and take in the atmosphere. E always managed to get me on the dance floor and we would dance and enjoy each other. When we were in our zone it seemed like there was no one around but us, our chemistry was electrifying. With him by my side I was able to let my hair down and truly let go of the responsibility and the stress —I could finally enjoy myself. E was so streetsmart and I knew he could handle himself and I in any arena, so I never thought twice about having a good time; for some reason I knew I was safe with him and I had never felt that secure and comfortable in my life.

I've never dreamt so much in my life, besides the nightmares, but now I was dreaming dreams filled with hope and possibility. We would sit up in the bed at night and just talk about life. We laughed till the sun would rise and I would call out of work some days just so it didn't have to end. It felt like two kids living a very grown up life, yet there were other times when we would have to put on our professional hats and we transformed into the conservative mature couple. It was amazing how there were no depths of me that E couldn't compliment; it truly seemed to me that we were two halves of a whole. He would rub my head to put me to sleep, and with each stroke I felt as if my mind was being cleansed of all the nosey thoughts and confusion; for a moment there was total harmony and peace of mind.

I was so proud to be his wife. It seemed like the best decision I had ever made; that was until— the parties were over and real married life started, and it was everything but fun. It became pretty obvious that we both had no idea what we were involved in. I learned quickly that there was one place E couldn't follow me, one place where he just couldn't have my back and that was in the real world; where the beautiful fantasy was often replaced with the ugly truth— that it would take a lot more than friendship to survive.

CHAPTER 7

Measuring Up

THE PROBLEM WITH trying to measure up to others' expectations is that you are always subjected to the opinion of a ruler; and if that ruler is man and not God, you will always come up short.

Reality quickly set in after the wedding. It was a struggle just to accomplish the simple things—things that I thought came naturally when you are in love. It's uncomfortable to admit, but I had to ask for things like hugs and kisses, and they never came easy. E didn't like it when I invaded his space with too much touchy-feely affection and intimacy. I guess he figured it would lead to me wanting to have sex, and he was never in the mood. The effects of our trying marriage were starting to show. I would get such bad nosebleeds arguing with E about my needs and how they meant nothing to him. I became so disgusted with myself as a result of his dissatisfaction with me. He didn't want to touch me or even be intimately close to me very often. I was young and married to a man who had no sexual attraction to me. I don't think I ever factored in that part being a struggle when I agreed to marry him; everything happened so fast that I don't think I factored in much about what everyday life would consist of.

We would make love once a month sometimes, and even then we struggled to find that connection. It seemed like he was doing it for me, like a job, not like a man enjoying his wife. I felt so nasty, like I was forcing him to do something he didn't want to do. Then he would have his spells where he would be all over me for about a week, then I would become invisible again. I would often have to ask for sex, and even then I was ridiculed and called nasty. He claimed sex was all I thought about. He told me he wasn't aroused because my hair and nails weren't always done and I didn't have on some sexy pajama set. I was always so scared of rejection that I never felt confident enough to do special things like that. He said it would help him receive me better, but I didn't believe him. He would physically smack my hand every time I tried to touch him in an intimate way. I wanted to cry many times, but I was too embarrassed to show I was hurt.

My confidence was completely gone, and I felt it was best to just continue to ask and wait until he felt like being bothered. I would beat myself up constantly, and I blamed it on my weight. I felt so uncomfortable walking around my own house without being fully covered. I could never get dressed in front of him, not fully naked, because I knew he would be watching. He looked at me with such disappointment; I knew he wasn't happy with me. I tried to diet, but I felt so defeated that I thought to myself, *Why even bother*? I kept gaining weight, and each pound felt like a chain wrapped around my neck. I felt trapped, discouraged, and ugly. It's amazing the effects one person can have on your self-worth when you give them power over your self-esteem.

I struggled with infertility, and I stopped getting my menstrual cycle on a regular basis at the age of sixteen. E wanted me to get pregnant so badly, but it just wouldn't happen. I wanted nothing more than to have his baby. I thought that if I could give him a child, it would validate him as a man and he would have a reason to be a committed husband. I thought it would make him love me, cherish me, and want to be around more; but I couldn't get pregnant. I took all kinds of medicines and nothing worked. I felt like I was worthless; like I wasn't a woman. I just couldn't make him happy no matter what I did.

I was constantly under a microscope and it was the worst in church. He would watch me to see how I responded to everything, how many hallelujahs I said, did I stand or clap my hands, was I a picture-perfect woman of God to his standards. He wanted so much of the drama, the fake show that many of the girls our age and older like to put on in church. I just wanted to be me and not feel obligated to follow some sort of checklist he created. I soon realized that very few things were genuine about E. We were in a make-believe world he created.

Times often got hard financially; I was the only one working most of the time, and I couldn't keep up with the life he wanted to live. He would often talk to me like I was a deadbeat husband who couldn't take care of his wife. I was so confused and hurt. I wanted nothing more than to make him comfortable and happy, hoping he would one day return the favor. I felt like he was trying to strip me of my femininity, forcing me into a position I could not fill—and when I couldn't, things got bad. E was the type of person who refused to go without his necessities, so I wasn't surprised when he decided to revert back to his former line of work in order to make some fast money. I never thought he would do this again. I thought it was over once we got married, but I soon found out the hard way—that E wanted what he wanted and would do anything to get it.

It started on a Saturday night. We had no money and I had to get to work that Monday. I was working at a small daycare center at the time and they were very strict about attendance. I couldn't risk losing my job, so E went out for a few hours and brought home a bag filled with wigs, makeup, and clothes. I knew what he was going to do. I tried to tell him not to do it, but he would look at me and simply say, "You got to go to work, right? And we got to eat, right? So do you have the money to make it happen?" and I reluctantly replied, "No." I felt so defeated and helpless, but he was right. I didn't have any way of getting the money, so I just went and sat down in the bedroom while he got dressed to leave. I always thought he was prostituting out there with those "clients," but he always told me he used his gift of gab to get what he wanted. I never really knew if he was telling me the truth about what he did out there all hours of the night, half dressed; the thought made me sick. I would never sleep until he came home, no matter how late it was. I would vomit and have the worst stomach cramps until he walked in the door safe and sound. I remember checking his body for marks or bruises that he might try to hide from me. My worst fear was that someone would discover he was a man and kill him.

Of course, it started out as one night just for food and work money, and turned into every other weekend. We always needed something: rent, money for church, food, or just pocket change. E hated to be broke. There was nothing I could say; love it or hate it, this was my life. When we were younger I thought nothing of it, but eventually watching him makeup his face, wearing those wigs and trashy clothes, it all began to mess with my mind. I watched my husband transform into the woman I could never be. In a matter of minutes, his whole spirit changed; his walk, his voice, even his facial expressions and his gestures changed. He was fierce and confident in that skin. He would play R&B music and parade around the house like a different person. He said it was a part of him getting into character so that no one would be able to expose him, but I knew he got some sort of high from it. I resented this fictitious woman who came to taunt me oh so often. I remember thinking to myself, *Is this who he wishes he was married to?* I watched as she buried my husband under her Mac makeup and cheap lingerie. Even now I have to remind myself that it was E all along.

He started wanting to make love more often when he had to go to "work." I guessed it made him feel better about the situation; but nothing was better. Everything seemed to be falling down a bottomless pit. I watched as my morals and values slipped through my fingers. I couldn't stomach the idea that I had to share my husband with anybody who had a car and a hundred dollars. There was no sanctity, and honestly it felt like there was no marriage. I was spinning in a whirlwind of deception. I shook hands with his friends who could be clients and clients who could be friends. I trusted nothing and no one, not even my husband. I thought it couldn't possibly get any worse. But I was wrong.

CHAPTER 8

Fighting for My Life

Blessed be the Lord, my rock, who trains my hands for war, and my fingers for battle. Psalms 144:2

IF OUR RADICAL relationship wasn't enough to convince me that this was no walk-in-the-park marriage, then spending our first wedding anniversary alone was a clear sign. It was the first of many holidays and momentous occasions I would be bringing in solo. I was "married single." I had the idea of being married, the burden of carrying another person, and the ring as a constant reminder that I was married, but ninety percent of the time I woke up alone.

The abuse became my only indicator that he was even in the house with me. The more I needed him, the angrier he became. I felt he was mad at me for pulling on him emotionally and forcing him into a role he didn't want to fulfill. I was in the way of what he really wanted to do and who he really wanted to be; that was obvious in the way he was so short with me. He had no patience for anything.

He would attack me so viciously at times. It was like I was paying for something that had nothing to do with me.

The worst feeling in the world is being hit by the man you love. There are no words to describe the powerless, weak, and sometimes compromising thoughts that run through you—you're never the same, and all it takes is one time. You try to go back in your mind to that free-flowing trust and love you had for the man that once meant the world to you, but you can't go back. That memory won't let you forget it.

I think back on the first time E hit me, and I can't seem to understand why I stayed, why I didn't run, heed the warning, and never look back. To this day I can't put my finger on what triggered the argument that day, but I can remember the sound of voices talking over one another, both wanting to be heard. E would state his piece and then sit back and listen with this look on his face, like a time bomb waiting patiently to explode. As I stared into his eyes I recall thinking, *this argument is really not that bad. Why is he so mad?* But I kept talking, analytically breaking down my point of view, hoping he was hearing me. He didn't hear me at all. A small argument about your typical relationship issues turned into an unstoppable rage and one of the most humiliating experiences of my life.

Right In the middle of my ranting and raving, E got up from where he was sitting and walked towards the closet. I figured he was going for his coat; he often walked out when the conversation got too real and he couldn't handle it. I jumped up and followed him, still stating my claim, but he wasn't going for his coat at all. His back was turned and I couldn't see what was coming. Then out of nowhere I saw his arm pull back as if he was taking something apart; he pulled out one of his belts, folded it, and turned towards me. I was so caught up in what I was saying that I didn't see it coming. He stood in front of me, similar to the way you would threaten a child, with one arm in the air holding the belt. His exact words were "So, you want to keep talking?" I couldn't help but feel like a child, but my pride wouldn't let me shut up; besides, I knew he was just trying to scare me. I opened my mouth to ask him what he thought he was going to do with the belt, but before I could get out a word, he swung the belt. I lifted my hands to block it, and it slapped me across my fingers. I wanted then to throw up my white flag and surrender, my hands burning from the sting, but my pride wouldn't let me. I screamed to him, "Are you crazy? "It was as if he didn't even hear me. He had an agenda and he wasn't going to stop until it was fulfilled. He swung that belt back and forth across my legs, arms, and hands. I stood there fighting back my tears, yelling, "E, stop!" I couldn't let him break me or bring me to my knees. I tried to back away, but he followed me. I could feel my spirit breaking, and perhaps that hurt more than the lashes of the belt. I tripped over a bag of clothes, my hand waving in the air, trying to break my fall as I hit the floor. When that final whip hit my thighs, I felt that barrier inside me crumble, and I could no longer hold back the tears. One tear fell down my face, and I quickly raised my bruised hand to wipe it away before he could see, but that one tear made way for a face full of tears. I couldn't believe what was happening to me.

E dropped the belt on the floor, got his coat, and stormed out the door. As I heard the front door slam, I struggled to get up, but when I stood to my feet, I knew I had left a piece of me lingering on the floor. I went to the bathroom, locked the door behind me, and ran a hot bath. I sat in the water, looking at my body—red, welted, and bruised. The water stinging my skin, I held my head down in shame, using my wash cloth to drown my face in water, and I cried as I often did when I was alone and there were no eyes watching.

He came home late that night, and neither of us spoke a word. The next day he got up early and left the house. He came back around dinner time with a bag that he dropped on the bed next to me; it was a sandwich from our favorite deli. As he turned and walked away, he said, "You see how I always think about you?" I couldn't understand what he meant by that, but I didn't want to waste the time trying to figure it out. I just needed something to take away the heavy, dark cloud that seemed to follow me. I was ready to make up. I hated the tension in the house, not speaking, feeling out of place in my own home; I swallowed what little pride I had left and said thank you and somehow I managed to gather a smile. He popped in a movie and I guess we were good again. I had hoped that would be the first and last time, but it wasn't. His wrath got more vicious, his punishments more extreme, and his patience shorter.

One of my most hurtful memories derived from one of our most vicious fights. E and I hadn't been speaking to each other for about two weeks. I was tired of walking around like a stranger in my own house, and if I walked into a room, he would go to another. The couch became his permanent sleeping quarters and I slept alone. I had enough, so I got up the nerve to walk into the living room, where he was watching a movie. I stood directly in front of the television and started talking. I was determined to be heard. I was going on and on about how ridiculous he was behaving. I knew there was a chance that he would attack me, but I was praying that for once we could just talk about what was happening in our relationship. I had to get some things off my chest. I figured if he was going to leave me then we might as well stop beating around the bush and get it all out in the open.

Without warning he got up and charged at me. I immediately tried to brace myself; I knew he was going to do this. Despite my efforts, he grabbed me by my neck and wrestled me to the ground. I fought back the best I could, but I was no match for his rage. I fell to the ground flat on my back and with both hands he dug into the scalp of my head and filled the palms of his hands with my hair. He dragged me from the living room, through the dining room, past a small hall into the doorway of our bedroom. I can remember how I screamed; trying to stop him by holding on to the edges of each door we passed. When we got to the bedroom, he yanked his hands free of my hair and left me lying there crying my eyes out in pain. I remember hearing him in the background telling me to get up, that I was so dramatic. He said, "You started it—now you want me to pity you? " He came back over to me and pulled me up aggressively.

I don't exactly know what I hit, but my back was so sore. I sat in the bed with my head spinning. I managed to get up and go to the bathroom to check my head; it felt like it was bleeding all over. As I looked in the mirror, tears rolled down my face. My hair was all over my shoulders and falling down my shirt. I went to touch a piece and it was coming out from the roots—one piece after the next just dropped into the bathroom sink. Before I knew it I had a sink full of hair. I was hysterical. I grabbed a scarf to wrap my head and ran for the phone, but I didn't know who to call. I couldn't call my family because I didn't want them to know that they were right, things were as bad as they seemed. I couldn't bring myself to call the police because I feared what would happen to E if he ever had to spend the night in jail. So I sat there with the phone in my hand and no guts to call anybody.

It took weeks for me to be able to use a brush or to comb through my hair. I couldn't understand how you could love someone and do the things he did to me. I was his wife, a reflection of himself. How could he do these things to me? I quickly learned exactly who I was married to, and his true colors became hard to ignore. He didn't want a wife. He was infatuated with marriage that was for sure; it was all he knew his whole life; it was a badge of honor. He was more in love with the status of being viewed as a married family man however; he wasn't concerned with fulfilling his duty as a husband to his wife. Everything seemed so insincere. He loved to showboat in church, walking around with his head held high like nothing was wrong, but outside of those church walls, I don't think he cared how I felt or what he did to me; he was in a world of his own.

The only time E was compromising or happy was when we had a little money— then he would want to be friends. He would go out and buy champagne, light candles, and play soft music in the house. He would move throughout the house like he was on a cloud, showering me with soft kisses on my shoulders as he passed me. If you didn't know any better, you would think he had the best marriage in the world. E was so good at sweeping me off my feet when he wanted to. He knew just what to say and what to do to create the fantasy, but the dream never lasted too long, and before I had the opportunity to get comfortable, he would start making his demands. He always had a long list of wants, everything from new clothes, jewelry, cars—you name it, he needed it. It was impossible to keep up with his material world, but I always tried to get him something nice every once in a while. It was never enough. Just when I thought I made progress, he would create something else; my efforts never counted for much. We would still argue and he would say with such conviction, "What do you do for me? You don't do anything for me," and in one sentence my efforts were discarded like garbage.

He would rather be anywhere but home, so I got used to not having his presence around. He packed up and left me so many times that I began to predict it before it happened. He would leave and then come back; I suppose when things weren't going too well with one of his lovers. He would constantly manipulate me with the fact that he was still my husband and that the Bible stated that I would be considered an adulterer if I ever moved on with someone else. Yet in his head, his sleeping with men didn't count as a sin, as long as he never slept with another woman. He was always saying things like that —one set of rules for me and another for him. He was so good at picking me apart. Laying my flaws on the table was an easy task, and he never held back. The trouble was, when it came time for him to turn the tables on himself, it was virtually impossible. In his mind he was the perfect husband, lover, and friend. I quickly realized I was nothing more than a small piece in his big puzzle.

CHAPTER **9**

Giving Up & Letting Go

The blessing of the lord maketh rich, and he addeth no sorrow with it. Proverbs 10:22

THAT SCRIPTURE WOULD play in my head constantly since the time I first read it. E believed that he was the best I could ever have, but this scripture showed me the true nature of God's blessing. I guess it gave me hope that one day things were going to be all right.

The hardest thing I ever had to do was realize that the man I met, full of love and life in high school, was not who I was dealing with. I knew E bore a spirit that hated me and hated him even more. It pushed me away, and when I refused to leave, it attacked me with a vengeance. I had to make a choice: to live or to die. I never wanted to leave him behind. I really didn't think I had it in me to do it. Even as I write these words retelling this story, I can't help but thank God for his grace and mercy. It was God's divine purpose over my life that wouldn't let me die in the midst of my mess. I began having nightmares of E killing me in the house; waking me up all hours of the night. I knew I had to go or something terrible was going to happen.

In May of 2009 I got up the courage to finally divorce him. He didn't put up much of a fight. I had to take the papers to him personally to get him to sign them. He looked at me with what appeared to be hurt in his eye and told me to leave the papers with him; he would mail them back for me. After he said that, we both stopped and looked at each other, and we knew it was over—or at least I did. I asked him again to please sign the papers and he did. Despite how he seemed hurt, I was sure this divorce was exactly what E wanted. He never wanted to be viewed publicly as the evil husband who divorced his wife, so he made things so bad that I would have no choice but to do it myself.

The divorce was done, but we were far from over. I soon learned that the one flesh I had created with E was not easily broken. It felt like I was undergoing surgery; each connecting piece of my heart and my mind had to be separated from him skillfully by God. It felt like the slightest wrong move could have cost me my life. I know he must have felt it too. Even after the divorce was final, his attempts to reconcile became a yearly routine. Out of them all, there was one time that I thought we might've had a chance.

I lost my job and I was unable to maintain an apartment after the divorce, so I was living with my sister at the time. I would often have to stay with her when I had to leave my house. Back and forth I would move my things, humbling myself as I went from being the woman of my own home to sharing a bunk bed with my nephew. I remember crying at night because I didn't have my own money to buy myself a stick of deodorant if I needed. I had to depend on my sister to provide for me. It was new for me, to say the least, and although she never made me feel bad about it, I couldn't stand being so vulnerable. I was so embarrassed. I never thought I would be able to forgive E for leaving me like that, never coming to see if I needed anything or just to slip a five dollar bill in the mail for me, just to preserve my dignity in front of my sister. It was obvious he didn't care.

It had been about six months and I started working part time. I managed to save a little extra money to get my cell phone turned on again, and it wasn't long before I got a call from E. He stayed on the phone with me for hours, telling me how God had truly delivered him this time; he claimed to have seen the error of his ways, and he wanted to take his place with his wife and try for his family. It all sounded good on the phone, often the way it had always sounded when conviction would set in and he would get a burst of passion for rebuilding our broken marriage. He invited me to meet a bishop that he had connected with. He told me the bishop was hosting a dinner for couples, and E didn't want to go alone.

Everything in me was telling me to hang up the phone; we were divorced. A piece of me really wanted to come up with some sarcastic line and hit him where it hurts, but my mouth opened and I told him I would come. The whole time I felt very awkward. We were surrounded by married couples talking about marriage and I felt out of place. This was our first time seeing each other after the divorce, and it was very uncomfortable.

I did get the opportunity to learn a lot about the bishop that night. He had an obvious gift to preach the gospel. At the time I didn't know what it was, but something about him just didn't sit well with me. I was always watchful of E when it came to pastors and men of clergy. As a child growing up in the church and battling with homosexuality, he would share stories about how his attempts to seek counsel from pastors and other men of authority in the church often turned into sexual advances; they would manipulate him into performing sexual favors, and some even held secret relationships with him. So instantly when he told me about this bishop I was skeptical. Months after the dinner I kept in contact with E and his progress shocked me. He went back to school for a nursing program and was approaching completion. He was even considering ministry, finally using his testimony to help others. I must say I was proud of him. He was doing well, and he had such a look about him—it was soft and innocent, and for the first time I felt like we might have a chance to salvage our marriage. The bishop offered to mentor E for ministry and told me that he was going to take E under his wing like the father he never had and teach him how to be a better man and husband to me. I was so filled with hope. We had never tried this before; E was never a fan of attending counseling, and after all we had been through, I knew God was our only resort.

Things seemed okay at first, although I did find some things very suspicious about this bishop. For example, he spoke of his wife as if she was the devil himself, complaining that she was an unholy woman. I was stunned to find out he had only been married a year. When I met his wife, I was shocked. She was a very unclean and unkempt woman. I asked myself how he could have married a women like this willingly just a year ago. Eventually I asked him about it, and he admitted he got her pregnant a few years back and he wanted to make a wrong situation right. He had a way with words, and he had mastered how to use the word of God to cover his sins, but there was a chunk of the story missing. Beyond my doubts, my desire to get E some spiritual guidance blocked my better judgment.

About a month after the bishop began mentoring E, he presented him with a dilemma. He told E that he was having trouble with his wife again, and he would need a temporary place to stay. When I spoke with the bishop about my concerns with him moving in with E he assured me that this was nothing less than a move of God. He said having this one-on-one time with E could only help him. I must admit I thought it wouldn't be too bad having a bishop living in the house with him, especially since I no longer lived there. I thought of it as around the clock surveillance.

Once he moved in, I would stop by the house every day to check in with E and to see how things were going. Whenever I came around, I saw nothing but good things happening. The bishop had a very authoritative way about him, and it seemed as if he wasn't letting E get away with anything. He made him throw away all of his female clothing that he used for work in the past. He constantly had E studying the Bible. I was so grateful that I even volunteered my assistance in helping the bishop with his plans to reopen his church building. Things for us never looked so bright. The bishop was very strict on us about not having sex until God revealed the time was right for us to get remarried. I had such a respect for him; it seemed he was putting so much into E that he didn't have the time to work on his own marriage.

Two months had passed and the bishop was still staying with E. I thought to myself it was strange that he didn't call his wife very often, nor did he go to visit her or their daughter, but I was secretly floating on a cloud of possibilities and I never addressed it—until I noticed a change in E's behavior. He got real quiet and at times he seemed like he was in a trance. I got worried and when I brought it up to the bishop, he told me that E was in spiritual warfare. He said E was being spiritually oppressed by a demonic entity. He assured me that he was in control of the situation, and when the time was right he would cast the spirit out of him. The bishop said it was the same spirit that used to cause him to beat on me when we were married. I was so afraid. I had no idea how to handle such a situation; I had no choice but to trust the bishop.

I continued to visit daily, and I noticed the bishop seemed to be getting a bit annoyed. He pulled me to the side and said that God had to do some work with E, and I was interfering by coming over so often; he told me that now was not the time for emotions and thinking on relationships, and by visiting so often, I caused E to lose focus. I was disappointed to hear that. I didn't think I was that much of a distraction. It was the first time we actually wanted to see each other and had a good time talking about future goals. I didn't want to stop coming over, so I started visiting less—about three times a week—and each time I came over, the bishop would recommend that I leave when the sun would set. He told us it was inappropriate for me to stay any later. So E would walk me to the bus stop every visit. I was starting to feel left out and a little disrespected. They were living in the house we occupied as a married couple. It still felt like home to me, and to have someone tell me to stay away didn't sit well.

After a few weeks of this I couldn't take it anymore. I came over one afternoon determined to have a long, hard talk with this bishop; instead, when I got to the house, he was sleeping, so E suggested we go for a walk in the park across the street. It was there that E finally told me what was going on. He and the bishop had been sleeping together the whole time. I felt so betrayed. My first instinct was to go upstairs and confront the bishop face to face. I got up from the park bench and raced upstairs. I stormed in the apartment door, and as it slammed behind me, it woke up the bishop. I looked him in his eyes and simply said, "Your assignment here is done. You are no longer needed." He looked at me, shocked, and proceeded to say, "What is going on here?" I knew he was lying. He knew why I was upset. E spoke up and told him that I knew what was going on. He replied, "She knows what?" I yelled out, "I know you've been sleeping with my husband!" The bishop looked at E and said calmly, "You didn't tell her everything." The bishop directed his conversation toward me and said "E and I have been in a relationship from the beginning, and he used the idea of mentoring him as a cover-up."

I was so lost. Millions of thoughts and moments ran through my head and I saw all the lies coming together at once. E instantly said the bishop was a liar they were never in a relationship. The bishop continued to tell me how he never wanted me involved, but I wouldn't go away and he took an unexpected liking to me. He said that he was trying to help E get over homosexuality, but until they both got delivered, it was best that if he slept with anybody, it should be him. I was sick to my stomach. I remember looking that bishop in his eyes, telling him that he would go to his grave trying to reopen his church; I told him that God would never allow it to come to pass until he got himself together. Before I could finish my next sentence, he grabbed a knife that was lying on the table and ran toward me. I thought I was going to die right where I stood. I had nowhere to run. I just stood still, staring him in his eyes the entire time. E jumped in front of me and fought him for the knife, and I used that opportunity to go and call the police.

That night after everything calmed down, I just sat in our old bedroom, stuck. I couldn't move. I just kept thinking, how could he allow this? I felt so violated. This bishop laying hands on me, praying prayers that I would keep myself and wait on my husband; and all the while he was sleeping with him. E never ceased to amaze me, but with this one, he created a new low. How could he expose my spirit to a man who clearly hated me and had no good intentions? I tried to ask E what in the hell he was thinking. He looked at me with tears in his eyes and said "I don't know what happened. It was like I was not myself. I just can't explain it." I turned my head and continued to stare out the window. I didn't have the energy to go any further with the conversation. I was just grateful to be alive.

I stopped going to church for a while after that. My anxiety got the best of me. I felt like every pastor was living a double life, and it made me sick to my stomach. I vowed never to be under the leadership of a man who could be anything like E or the bishop he slept with. My life was a mess and I just couldn't get a break. I was being attacked on all sides.

I never wanted to see the bishop's face again, and I sure didn't want him to contact E again. So, I moved back in with him, trying to make sure the bishop didn't return. I hoped he could go back to the way he was before the bishop came to stay. But he never went back to that person. He started to behave very weird, almost spooky. He would sit in front of a blank blue television screen for hours just staring into it. Sometimes he would go get a bag of marijuana and blast some gospel music while he smoked it. I had never seen this side of him before. If E respected no one, he knew never to play with God like that. It was the one thing he never mixed; his nonsense with God's business. Something was so different. He would walk around treating me like I was pure evil, as if I was in on some plot to hurt him. He stopped eating anything I cooked and accused me of praying to idols over his food. I couldn't figure out where this was coming from. He stopped speaking to me, he never wanted to leave the house, and he would just sit in the bedroom reading the Bible from the time he got up to the time he went to sleep. I felt powerless. Something was going on—something deeper than anything I had ever experienced. I didn't know what to do to help him. I couldn't help myself.

He did this for a while and then he kicked me out, in so many words. He gave me a choice, I could move out or continue to live in the house, but we would not be together and he would be free to do as he pleased. Needless to say I decided to take his invitation to move out and I took only the clothes I could gather together and left most of my things behind. As I packed my bag and gathered my things, E sat in the room yelling out loud Bible scriptures at me, laughing to himself, saying that I was going to get what was coming to me. I rushed quickly to leave; I was so frightened and it was so eerie. How could he have thought for a second that I was some kind of devil in disguise when I was the only person who had been there for him? I sacrificed everything.

I later heard from a friend, who visited the apartment after I moved out, that he threw out all our furniture and clothes and he even threw out all the food in the refrigerator; all of it was lying on the side of the building. My friend told me she saw people from the neighborhood picking over it as they took what they wanted.

As for me, it was back to my sister's house, and she was expecting me. My health began to show the proof of my life's anguish. My menstrual cycle had stopped completely, and the idea that I would never be able to have children devastated me and created a cold and bitter place in me. I rarely smiled; I had nothing to smile about. The weight gain was so rapid that I had to go to a specialist, and I was diagnosed with Polycystic Ovarian Syndrome, which explained my constant battle with weight, infertility, and depression. I remember the day I came home from the doctor's office with a pamphlet on the disease and I sat in the bathroom and began to read all the symptom, hair loss, facial hair growth, obesity, depression, anxiety and infertility. I already struggled with feeling like a woman after all I had endured with E and then this —I felt like I was being punished and the worst part was that it was incurable. I fought to keep my head up. The medication I had to take just to try and control the symptoms, made me so sick and I was always weak and tired. Just when I thought I had nothing left I always got this feeling deep down inside of me that wouldn't let me give up, it actually gave me a second wind of strength and I didn't waste it. I pressed forward with all that was in me.

Just as I began to gain an inch of my strength back, E would find a way to come back to knock me down again, but I knew I couldn't put all the blame on him; for some reason I kept allowing it. This time he didn't call with his routine proposal of reconciliation; instead he cut right to the chase. He needed money. E and I had been divorced for over a year, and he had been living his life openly as a trans-sexual. He had no intention of working a regular nine to five, so his fast money often came and went on hair, nails, and clothes to fit the part. I knew what he was doing with his money, but he knew how to get me to give him mine. He would claim that he had no money for food; that he hadn't eaten in days. I would always give what I had whenever he needed money. After he got the money from me, he would be kind enough to answer my phone calls within the week, at least once or twice.

I know you're probably wondering why I would even call. And I wish I had an answer, but I don't. Each time I called, there would be no telling who would answer. I'd call hoping to hear the sound of his voice, and I was greeted by a female's voice. He changed everything. I could only imagine the amount of hormones he was using in order to change the sound of his voice. During phone calls I would attempt to call him E, and he would reply by saying, "I don't know anybody by that name." It would break my heart to hear him talk about himself like he was dead, even though that's what it felt like; like a death had taken place. I remember calling him on the phone just to call him a murderer. I would go on and on about how he was just killing the man I loved right before my eyes and there was nothing I could do about it. He would tell me that he was not a man and that the Lord told him he was a woman. It felt like somebody had just pressed erase and wiped away my whole life. The love I thought I had once upon a time only existed in my memories. I was so confused. I knew for sure this was it; he was never going to change. We had not seen each other in over a year, and we had not spoken in months.

The next time I heard from E, he was back to his old tricks. He called me, crying like a baby; I could hardly understand him on the phone, because he was so hysterical. He told me how much he couldn't live without me; that I was the only one he ever loved and how he wanted to change his life again. You would think that I would be sick of hearing that line over and over again, but E always managed to pop up and catch me at a weak point. I was tired of being lonely, and I had yet to start dating again. I had nothing else going on. Consciously I knew it was all lies, but I just needed something to happen in my life. He would come back to me, and each time I could see the effects of what he had done to himself. The hormones would break down his facial features and his bone structure, so with each visit, depending on the length of time we hadn't seen each other, it was like watching him slowly transform into a woman right before my eyes. I had so many mixed emotions, a weird combination of love and hate.

At the time he was living in an apartment around the corner from me, and he wasn't satisfied, so he was looking for something better, and an opportunity arose. He moved into the vacant apartment directly above mine. I had my doubts and I even tried to stop him at the last minute, but he said he thought it would be good for us; we would be able to see each other regularly and still have our space to take things slow. That all sounded good, and a week after he moved in, he bought some new clothes—male clothes—and got a haircut. He had changed the outside appearance, but this was nothing new; it was a part of the process I knew all too well, but the inside was still the same. I spent some money to furnish his apartment and buy some new things to add to his wardrobe. Yes, it was a stupid move, I know, but it was so hard for me to turn my back on him. About two weeks later he claimed he couldn't do it any more, he couldn't live his life as a man, and to no surprise he didn't want to have anything to do with me anymore. He said he wasn't being true to himself.

For two months I lived in hell. I watched as men came in and out of his apartment. I drove myself crazy trying to figure out which ones he was sleeping with. The sounds of them laughing and partying upstairs taunted me; my ear stayed glued to the apartment walls. The worst of it all was when I discovered that I could hear the squeaking from his bed at night as he had sex with his boyfriend right over my head!

Life was too much to bear. I was sliding down a slippery slope to self-destruction. I couldn't take the squeaking of the bed. Our bedrooms where aligned and I couldn't avoid it. I would bang the broom on the ceiling to get him to stop. I used to go to bed with headphones on to drown out the sounds, but it would cause swelling on the inside of my ears, and I knew that I couldn't keep it up for too long. I stopped sleeping in the apartment and I spent most of my time at my sister's house, too scared to go home. My nosebleeds came back stronger than ever, and I would bleed for almost an hour sometimes until I felt weak and I fell asleep. I just knew this was going to be it for me; I thought for sure that the spirit in E that taunted me and hated me was going to get its victory, and I was going to take my own life out of sheer desperation for peace. I had countless anxiety attacks.

I remember the day I sat on the edge of my bed listening to him and his boyfriend upstairs laughing while I was downstairs dying. I got lost in my own thoughts, and I noticed I lost something a long time ago. I don't know whether it got lost in my tears that I shed over my father's lifeless body or whether it was beaten out of me by E, or maybe it was stolen by all the trespassers who entered into my womb; but whenever it happened, however it happened, I've never been the same. I lost something. I lost the smile that would paint my face like watercolor. I lost my joy in the search, and I hadn't found anything. I don't know what I was looking for, and I wasn't even sure I didn't already have it. I lost something in the hype of it all. In the confusion of everybody else's dance, I lost my step. I lived in a glass house—seen but never touched. I had to have lost something because no one I've ever been challenged with was ever strong enough to steal, kill, or destroy what I lost. It was something I lost. I dropped it; set it down; let others borrow it. I lost my sight showing someone else the way.

As I sat at the edge of that bed, it was then and there that I was forced to try to understand my own struggle. I knew the reality of my own personal truth was too much to bear, but I knew I had to do it. If I didn't, I knew that would be the last day of my life. All at once, I could here the sound of E laughing, the sound of two men breathing in a sexual climax, I felt the weight of my siblings on my shoulders and legs, the burden of my mother on my chest, the disappointment in my belly and the wind from the open bedroom window smacking me in the face. It was either choose to live or jump out of my bedroom window.

On that February 14, 2010, Valentine's Day, sitting on the edge of my bed, I opened my eyes to see how far from myself I had allowed this life to take me. Then I stopped. I just stopped. Numbness fell over me. I fell to my knees and screamed from the pit of my belly; I screamed and I could finally hear me. That still, small voice grew to the size of ten thousand women wailing, and I didn't care who heard me. I felt the presence of the Holy Ghost all over me, and tongues fell from my lips like a gasp of air held in for too long. My day had come and my yoke was broken. I no longer had to pull the load. It was lifted with a single touch from God. It didn't matter anymore. None of it mattered anymore. I woke up on February 15th a changed woman. As I looked outside of my door that morning, I saw movers carrying boxes and bags out of E's apartment. He moved out that Monday morning, and that was the day God saved my life. I knew I had been set free from all the things that bound me, but deliverance is not magic; there is no magical touch that makes all the wrongs right. God showed me that night I could have a life that was not filled with disappointment and misery, but the true test was going to be taking him at his word even in adversity, believing with my whole heart that what God promised me would come to pass, no matter how long it took. That would be my greatest challenge.

CHAPTER 10

It's a Different World

I HAD MIXED feeling of happiness and sadness, for I knew that from here on out, I would be on my own. I grew a dependency on the drama between me and E. It had become my life, and now that it was over, I had nowhere to turn. My first thought at the time was to go crawling back to Truth, but I had come too far, and my pride wouldn't let me go back.

I would be lying to you if I said that after it was all said and done, I was free to live my life and all my troubles were over— the truth is it got more complicated. I had managed to spend the last thirty years of my life living in the shadows of others. I had no life of my own to live. I had always been what I needed to be to help somebody or to try and win somebody's heart, but that wasn't who I was at all. The harsh reality came when I realized that I still didn't know who I was. I knew what I was capable of, but I had no idea who I was. I had to ask myself hard questions like, who am I without all the influence and the direction from my ex-husband? Who am I without the responsibility of raising someone's children? Who am I without love? The answers to these questions didn't come easily. I had to fight through my pride and my blurred vision of reality and see the truth once and for all. I was so overwhelmed with all the thoughts that filled my head. But after deep reflection, I came up with this: I am E's ex-wife, I am my mother's crutch, I am my sibling's help, and I am my worst enemy. Once I released the truth, I wasn't happy with any of it. My world began to close in on me. I was boxed in by thoughts and thoughts and more thoughts.

I wondered about the simple things that women take for granted, the ability to develop your own expressive style; having my own vision that wasn't dictated by anxiety and fear of someone's approval. The freedom to be a woman, delicate and soft; I didn't want to be hard and cold, loud, high and mighty. I had no desire to be a warrior, fighting forever; I only wanted to be real, a unique design of a woman few have ever seen, with the ability to effectively take every part of me—past, present, and future—and become a work of art. But I was far from that woman in my dreams. I remember thinking to my self the night E moved out that what I needed to do was reinvent myself.

I decided to go out and buy some new clothes and get my hair done. Everything seemed to be looking up. The next morning I got up early, eager to start my day's journey of finding Shamina. I started with a little pampering and got a pedicure. When the woman at the nail salon asked me what color I wanted, I stopped and began to feel that feeling of anxiety come upon me as I stumbled to pick the color, worrying if I was going to pick a color that E would approve of or whether I was picking a color that others would think was nice. I had to stop myself from worrying about things that didn't matter. As the woman looked at me with anticipation, I quickly said black. The whole time I was in the chair, all I could think about was *What in the world are you going to do with black toes?* It was the first color that managed to fight its way through all the junk in my head and come out of my mouth, so black it was.

As the woman finished the pedicure and began to paint my nails, I closed my eyes, pretending to be resting when the whole time I was screaming on the inside. I wanted so bad to tell her to stop, but I just sat there still and seemingly calm. When she was done, she tapped me on my leg, and I opened my eyes, looked at my feet, and I almost wanted to shout. They were so beautiful to me. The glossy black paint shimmered next to my light brown skin; it was so unique, it was me. As I got up to sit in the chair to get my nails done, I could see women looking at my toes—as uncommon as they were, they were beautiful, and everybody noticed. I heard a woman whispering to her friend, "Her feet look really cute. I might try that one day." I know it may not seem like a big deal to many, but for me it was the first step in discovering myself, and I lit up inside and out. In the midst of all my glory, I couldn't help but notice a little girl no more than ten years old sitting in the seat next to me. The women doing her nails had gathered some colors that she thought the little girl would like. As the woman sat down in front of the little girl, she asked her, "Do you know what color you want?" and before she could get out another word, the girl said, "Yellow please" with such surety. The woman went on to say, "Yellow? Are you sure? I have a nice bubble gum pink," but the little girl interrupted her and said, "No thank you. I want yellow." Again I found myself in such a sentimental place as I watched this little girl, so small and fragile, do something that I was just now only attempting to accomplish. I was taken by emotion. I knew for sure that what I was going through didn't just happen because of my marriage; this was the effect of a lifetime of bad decisions. Never having the opportunity to choose to explore, I was always too busy playing it safe so that I could provide the consistency everybody expected from me. I left the nail salon that day in a wonder— so many ideas and even more thoughts.

I discovered that day that I was a woman of many different shades. I had to learn that femininity is not a fad or style; it just simply is. Femininity can be defined on so many different levels that it is impossible to box it in with one shallow definition. There were many days to follow this one, which helped me realize that it's okay not to be okay, that being vulnerable is not a weakness, but rather a gift; a unique opportunity to experience love and caring like never before. That night as I lay in my bed, I asked myself another one of those hard questions. "Who am I?" and I humbly whispered in the dark, "I am fashionable, empathetic, and wise; I am a ponytail to the back, sweat suit kind of girl just as much as I'm a diva."

Yes, it was a different world for me now that the dust had settled and I was all alone, but I like different, because "normal routine" never taught me or anybody anything. But different—now, that changes lives.

CHAPTER 11

New Life

It is a fact that after the abolishment of slavery, many of the freed slaves voluntarily remained with the slave masters who persecuted them; too afraid of what lay beyond the cotton fields, Some found jobs working on another plantation for pennies to do the same work as their previous slave master. But after years of oppression, some managed to fight their fears of change and growth, and they seized the opportunity for reciprocity, and they started new lives, filled with endless possibilities.

I ATTEMPTED TO move forward. My mind was made up. This time I planned to take my time. I wanted to take time to find myself and to allow someone the opportunity to truly get to know me. Before settling down with another man, I wanted to make sure I had lived for me first. I wanted to try and right the wrong decisions I had made in past relationships. I no longer wanted to settle for less or good enough—no, I wanted to make a sound decision concerning love that wasn't dictated solely upon emotions. My heart had proven to be untrustworthy, and I chose to use my head this time. I was still so insecure about my body, so I joined a gym just around the corner from me. I brought new furniture and curtains to shake things up a bit.

It had only been two days since I started my all-about-me movement, when on February 17, 2010; I received a phone call and a visit that would change everything. I received a call from an old friend named Wyatt. I knew him from my teenage years; he was a roommate to a friend of mine, back in high school. He had some interest in me back then, but it never got off the ground. And honestly there was always something about him that I thought was a bit weird. He was so shy and so quiet it seemed he was in a world all of his own. I remember calling him about a month before E moved into the building. I guess I was trying to take my mind off of E for one night and possibly entertain the idea of meeting someone new; so I guess this was a return phone call. I was shocked; I didn't expect to hear from him again. I mean, we didn't leave our conversations on a bad note or anything; it's just that it was one of those conversations you don't expect to go anywhere. He said I was on his mind and he wanted to know how my Valentine's Day was. I remember asking him how he knew Valentine's Day was one of my favorite holidays. I told him unfortunately it wasn't so great this year. I can still hear the sense of urgency in his voice as he responded, "Why didn't you call me? I didn't know that you were alone and you didn't get anything. I would have come to see you." It was refreshing to hear a man actually care about something I cared about, something concerning my needs. Lying through my teeth, I told him it was no big deal. He had to cut the call short because he was at work. But it was flattering in a way to have spoken to him.

I continued on with my day, and about ten o'clock that night my bell rang. I was reluctant to answer it, fearing it might be E coming back to start some mess, but something told me to answer the door. I called from the intercom to find out who it was, and a man's voice said, "Wyatt." I thought it was a joke. I had mentioned my address during our conversation once before, and I was shocked that he even remembered it. I put on some clothes and went to open the door. I was not prepared for what I saw on the other side. I turned the knob and opened the door to find Wyatt standing there, his hands filled with two dozen long-stemmed roses in a glass vase, a teddy bear, candy, and a gift bag. I thought I was dreaming. I stood there for a minute in disbelief. I had never had a man do something like this for me unless I knew about it and pretty much paid for it my self. But here was this man struggling to hold it all in his arms, presenting me with more than what I would have even asked for.

I stood there for what seemed like a minute and then quickly snapped out of my thoughts long enough to hear him say, "Can you give me a hand?" I laughed and quickly grabbed some things from him. When we got into the apartment, I had to fight to conceal my smile, which stretched from ear to ear. I said to him, overcome with emotion, "You didn't have to do all of this. " He looked at me and said, "Nah, I wanted to. You deserve it." For a moment I thought to myself, *Could this be God, some supernatural manifestation of God's love toward me?* How could he have known I deserved this? My heart —still bleeding from what took place just days ago; still managed to feel something in that moment, I hugged him and said thank you with such momentum behind it. I was thanking him for so much more than the gifts. I was thanking him for giving me hope. To think, just days ago one man could think I was nothing, and another could respect me more than I respected myself.

We talked for a while and I was still so taken by everything, but suddenly those thoughts in my head began to conjure up feeling of worry and anxiety again. I wondered, *why, why would he do all this for nothing?* I started to feel like I wanted to give it all back, I was scared. Our conversation had begun to die down, and the room grew still. I knew then that he was going to try and sleep with me. I wanted to tell him thank you and good night, but I had never had a man spend so much of his own money, and he didn't have to do this just for me, so I felt like I owed him something. So that night I let him spend the night with me. The whole time I couldn't help but to think *What am I doing?* I had gone from a married woman to this; a late-night lust over some roses, candy, and a teddy bear. I felt so bad, but I hid it from him as best I could.

The next day after he had left, I felt so ashamed. Once again I found myself wondering if this was a blessing or a curse. I know I said I was going to take my time and date, but this had gone too far to turn back now. I had hoped that he was just using me and I would never hear from him again after that night, but I was wrong; he called all the time to check on me. He came to visit me almost every day right after work, and every day turned into him spending every night with me. He was an amazing man, but I couldn't help feeling like he wasn't my amazing man —that one man that I felt like I couldn't live without. Sometimes I felt like he was a distraction, pulling me further away from myself and what I wanted, but one thing just kept leading to another, and I never wanted to hurt him. He was too good of a man, so just like that I was stuck in an unfulfilling relationship, trapped in a whirlwind of meaningless sex with a good guy. I felt horrible. I couldn't stop beating myself up with questions: *Why couldn't I love him? Why was I not feeling any connection? Why did I settle?* It pained me that I could love a man like E, but when presented with a guy like Wyatt, I just couldn't find the spark.

I'm surprised I stumbled upon Wyatt. I know our paths crossed for a reason at this point in both of our lives, where we stood in need of emotional Band-Aids. It was obvious with one look in his eyes, we were both so needy. *And why wouldn't I give it a try?* We were good, sincere, and hardworking people, and despite the lack of emotional sparks, I felt like I owed it to him to try and see if love would grow. I knew that if I wanted to throw myself into this relationship, I would have a good life. Wyatt would have given me anything I wanted and needed, but he couldn't give me those butterflies I was longing for. It may sound childish to you, but I knew what it was like to love someone so much that it wakes you up at night and forces you to watch them while they sleep. I have loved a man so deep that I was willing to make the impossible possible. I had experienced such a high off love that I just couldn't settle for good enough. It came down to one simple truth: I wasn't in love with Wyatt; I wanted to be, I had every reason to be, but I wasn't. He was full of love and patience. I never had a man desire me so much, and intimately he was so satisfied with me. I struggled to search my heart for anything I could grab on to that would help me love him the way he loved me, but I found nothing that would stick.

Wyatt had such a hard life and never really had the opportunity to be the independent man he is so destined to become. I guess I was just at a different stage in my life, and I was unable to waste any more of my time rescuing someone else. I felt like he was pulling on me, forcing me into this nurturing motherly role, not like my lover, but more like a child would cling to his mother. I instantly pulled back, terrified of what would happen if I allowed myself to compromise my life again to take care of another person's emotions besides my own. I had come so far and felt so many different emotions that I could no longer lie to myself. I knew we didn't have the chemistry and he was not the man for me, but he had the will of a hundred men and he weaned me back to life, bandaged me up the best he could, and showed me that all men are not created equal.

Once I came face to face with the reality of our relationship, I had to tell him; though it hurt me more than it hurt him to break his heart. I invited him over one night to let him know that this had to end. I told him how I felt about having sex and about not being in love; I told him what my plans were just before he came into my life; and I told him I wanted to slow down and possibly date each other without all the playing house, spending the night every night, and pretending to be this married couple that we weren't. I can remember telling him "Who knows what could happen in the future? Things may change," but he was not trying to hear a word I was saying. I couldn't believe how he just disregarded what I said; he looked at me with such a serious face as if he was about to cry and said "I don't want to stop coming over to the house. I like us the way we are. I don't want things to change." I was so uncomfortable; I had never had a man put me in such a position. I had never even seen a man show that much emotion, so I was lost. I tried to explain to him how much I needed this time for me to heal from some things in the past, but all he could focus on was how much he wanted me in his life, so being the old Shamina, I told him that I would give the relationship another try to make him happy. In a way I was hoping for a miracle; some unexpected burst of love for him that I might have neglected to feel. I was determined to give him the fairest chance I could, despite my obvious disconnection. I tried to give him the opportunity to win my heart. And as crazy as it may have seemed, I was secretly hoping he would be able to do it.

We stayed together for a year, and within that year I felt so alone, trapped, and unhappy, but he didn't notice anything. He managed to get me to give in to moving out of my apartment into an area that he was obsessed with; yes, I said obsessed. All he would do is talk about how much he hated the area I lived in and how great it would be for us if we moved. After about a hundred subliminal messages, I decided to give in. He did things like that often; he had a sort of manipulating way about him and he only saw what he wanted to see in his perfect world he created. And again I was a puppet in someone else's show.

About two months before my thirtieth birthday, I was on the phone with one of my high school girlfriends, and she was telling me how she started a new job, was working on her master's degree, and surprisingly she and her cheating ex-boyfriend got back together. I was not shocked by that news as much as I was moved by her reason. She said she decided to do what made her happy. When I hung up the phone, I began to think about what would make me happy. I had already been getting the pre-thirtieth birthday blues, but I asked myself, *am I doing what makes me happy?* And as I sat there with the phone still dangling in my hand, I knew the answer. I was miserable. I was reminded of how important it is to me that I find true love, how important it is to me that I find the true me, and by the end of my thoughts, I knew what I had to do. That night, long after the phone call, I could think of nothing else. Even in my dreams I was bombarded with thoughts spinning around my head. *What was I waiting for? Why was it so easy to live for everybody else but myself?* I couldn't take it anymore. I woke up, rolled over, and told Wyatt that I couldn't do it anymore.

He didn't take the breakup easily, and it was very hard for me at first, because once again I moved out of my apartment into a new apartment that I couldn't afford alone; so leaving meant going back to stay with my sister, who was now a newlywed. I was so disappointed in myself; that decision to give up my apartment was so out of character. I was back at square one, and to no surprise, I was laid off from my job as a substitute teacher. So staying with my sister on unemployment was the last place I thought I would have ended up. I had a plan and it all fell apart trying to make someone else's dreams come true.

Despite how things may have turned out, I thank God for Wyatt and truly believe one day when he gains the life experience that God is trying to give him, he will be a blessing to any woman who crosses his path. I never had to break somebody's heart before, and I never want to do it again. I still feel emotional when I think of him, but good or bad guy, I had to be honest with myself. I needed help. When we broke up, I had some time alone; it really helped me shed some light on just how difficult it was being with another man besides E. As I began to think back on the relationship with Wyatt, I realized I gave him such a hard time about a lot of things that were unnecessary, like the way he dressed for church, the way he spoke, the way he was so rough around the edges, and I began to realize that after dealing with E, I had no idea how to accept a "regular" man. I struggled to reconnect myself to the musk of a man; the essence of their normalness didn't sit well with me. I felt so out of place with the uncomfortable battle of masculinity and femininity; I had to remind myself what it was like to surprise a man with the simplicity of just being a woman. I used to get mad when Wyatt would tell me how beautiful I was, and I was always waiting to hear how my shoes didn't match perfectly with my outfit or how my hair wasn't done quite right but; he never spoke a word of discord to me, and I accused him of not paying attention to me, when he was just being a man. I needed help learning how to be a woman again. After all I had been through with E, I was confused. What was my role? In our relationship I found it hard to trust Wyatt to make decisions for me. I wanted to know everything; *how much the check was at dinner, how much gas was in the tank* —I was all mixed up. I wanted a good man to come and take control and let me rest, but I didn't know how to rest or how to relinquish my control into the hand of another.

After I broke things off with Wyatt, I understood where I went wrong. I was living with a man who was not my husband and trying to avoid the real problem —myself. I had to allow myself to feel everything and deal with each pain. I could no longer look for a place to hide them; I had to let them go. I gave up, but I was still holding on —so I started over again. The first thing I did was pull out a box that I had held on to for too long. I call it my box full of tears; it was filled with painful reminders of my life with E. In this box I had saved the hospital bracelets and the oxygen bags from the paramedics to remind me of every anxiety attack I had crying hysterically over E and our marriage. Every suicide attempt was recorded in this box, along with police reports and court papers acquired during my life with E. I held on to it as a reminder to insure that I would never, ever allow him back into my life again. I realized it wasn't Wyatt or that box that was going to keep him away or the haunting effects of our past together; it was my decision to be free that would truly help me to move past the old life I had and into the new life I wanted.

CHAPTER 12

Forgiveness

STARTING OVER AGAIN was rough. I was tired of trying and even more tired of failing. I thought that the answer was moving on to another relationship, but with every attempt, it only made me wonder if I would ever be able to love someone else without picking them apart. Memories of a life of lies were all I had to keep me company. I grew furious at the reality that everyone around me seemed to be elevating, smiling and loving, and I was trapped in a rerun of memories of a life of deception. I became enraged by every tear I cried, longing for a moment in the past that was nothing more than the good work of an actor. I began to feel the need to question if anything in my life was real. I just knew I had my breakthrough—the yoke had been broken— I knew it was, *so why did I still feel so unhappy?*

I noticed that there was a seed planted within me left behind by my ex-husband that was still doing his dirty work. I still couldn't get dressed to go to the store without picking myself apart. There were times that I would stay home for days because I didn't have my hair done, fearful that I might bump into him on the street; I couldn't bear for him to look at me like I was a letdown, incapable of taking care of myself without him. The anxiety was endless. I just knew I had dealt with my issues, *so why was I still hurting? Why was I creating this prison for myself in a room tucked away in the back of my sister's house, too ashamed to leave because of my weight?* I thought I had covered all my bases. *Why was I doing this to myself?*

With nothing but time to think and analyze my situation, I came to the conclusion that I had missed something very important: forgiveness. I wanted so bad to look like this mature woman who was healed and over it all, but I was lying to myself. I felt like everything I wanted to do just fell apart, and I always found a reason to blame E. I knew then that I had some unfinished business to handle. I had to keep it real with myself and admit to being another bitter, emotionally damaged, "angry woman." I allowed myself more time to honestly express how I was feeling, and to no surprise— I was pissed off!

I was so angry with E. I hated the fact that he gave up; in my eyes I felt like he chose that lifestyle over me. It was like he just stopped fighting. Most of all I hated the fact that he made me fear him. We used to find refuge in each other, and he tarnished that image I had of him. Thoughts of him now only brought up memories of pain, devastation and lies. We could never go back, and I knew that, but I hated the fact that I was alone. I thought maybe I was nothing without him, not worthy of love.

It was at this point that God began to show me just how bound I was. I had harbored this anguish, this resentment in my heart, and although I claimed to have moved on,

I was still married, frozen in time. I had to forgive E. I had to stop blaming him for my lack of enthusiasm and accomplishment. I was so accustomed to telling my sad story, leaving out my triumphant victory. I now know that if I had stayed in that frozen state, I would have never been able to see God in myself, in my life, and in my testimony. It took time to truly forgive and forget, but the more I found myself in the presence of God, seeing me through his eyes, the more I became passionate about ministry. I found joy and I learned that I can have a personal relationship with God without being led or ushered into his presence by my ex-husband. I know now that I can seek God for myself.

God had to teach me how to forgive in order for him to make me over again without the doubt left over from the chaos. I had to find myself and prepare myself for greatness. Once I began to heal and see a future before me, I wanted so many things, and no less grateful was I that God spared my life and my sanity. Now that I was out of the situation and able to see things as they were and not as I wanted them to be; I needed more. I wanted my smile back, my freedom, my hope; I wanted my peace back and most of all I wanted the years back and the time wasted.

I am now a thirty-year-old woman who has been married and divorced and has loved countless people but never truly loved herself. So I am not shocked that at thirty years old I have had sex with a man, but never made love to one before, for I know few who have ever been so lucky. The way I see it, many of us touch without feeling and we pour into each other from empty glasses, so I know I'm not alone in my reality. I accept that it's from my heart and my imperfections that my desires for true love manifest. I may not know what it's like to feel the passion of an even exchange, a lover's kiss, a spiritual connection, oneness, and yet I stand in the middle of my circumstances like a city set on a hill, unable to hide, the desires of my heart dangling from my sleeve, exposed. I stand boldly in front of an audience of spectators, thanking the Lord that I didn't fall. Humble and proud at the same time, I'm destined to make it out of my wilderness, and I have to believe there is a land out there —somewhere, filled with milk and honey, waiting for me.

Sometimes I feel so close to my dreams that I can taste it. I know now that I am a chosen woman; designed for a great work, and as I reflect back on my life, I realize that I had been only a character in one of the most epic love stories ever told. I am God's beloved and he was so jealous and so persistent to gain my trust and win my heart that he allowed man to break it so he could put it back together again. I have strength and destiny running through my veins I can't lose and I have made the conscious decision to be free from death, addiction and self pity. Through my perseverance I have destroyed the generational cures that has crippled my ancestors simply because I refused to die

Occasionally I still have to remind myself that my happy ever after is never going to come true with E. The hardest thing I ever had to do was let go of the dream and stop waiting for God to perform a miracle and recognize— he already has. I write this book from a humble place of understanding, maturity, and authority that I never thought I could possess. God's will was done. And make no mistake, even as I write these words I struggle with feelings of shame and loneliness, but I accept it. I embrace my vulnerability, the many pieces of me, good and bad. I learned how to love and how to protect my most prized possession—my destiny.

After it all —the fights, the tears, the joys, the disappointments; I can say with confidence that somebody loved me, somebody somewhere prayed for me, and God made intercession for me and preserved my heart, mind, body, and spirit for someone and something glorious.

Indeed a city set on a hill cannot be hidden; so now I happily tell my story, accepting the fact that I may become the object of ridicule and judgment. I welcome the opportunity to become the center of conversation around your dinner tables and the gossip of your congregations; it is all worth it to show somebody that it can be done. You can shake yourself loose of the things that don't belong to you, the emotional baggage, insecurities, and inadequacies of others that you picked up along the way, and it doesn't have to take thirty years to do it. It took thirty years for me to become interested in myself, thirty years to be able to begin to fall in love with me, and thirty years to learn how to let go of the pain, shame, and the fear— and just chase my dreams. I am one of the lucky ones. So many people get swallowed up in the cycle of fighting everybody else's battles except their own— never, ever breaking free to live life for themselves.

During one of my seminars at a local college in my area, a man asked me one of the most honest and powerful questions I have ever been asked. He said, "What would the Shamina of today say to the Shamina of yesterday?" and before I answered him, I took a deep breath and remembered that tough little girl carrying the weight of the world on her shoulders, walking the streets of the Bronx dragging her siblings to school, and with such ease I answered, "I would tell her to keep her head up because it will all come together one day and she will finally be able to just rest."

I struggled with the decision to write these words that you now read because a piece of me felt like there was no happy ending, no fairy-tale story of Prince Charming coming in and sweeping me off my feet. There is no Mr. Right waiting to fix all the wrongs others have done. I struggled with the idea that everybody would expect to read about a "happy ending" and I am still single, still waiting for true love, but I realized that my story wasn't a fairy tale but rather an example of real life. I don't have a happy ending, but I was given a new and happy beginning. I took the journey few women ever get the courage to take. I went back into Pandora's box, gathered up all the pieces of me I had left behind in the hands of the men I once loved, and placed them in a basket labeled Shamina—and God put them back together. Now I proudly wear my scars like a badge across my chest that reads:

"All things work together for the good of them that love God and are called according to his purpose." - Romans 8:28 (KJB)

Acknowledgments

Thank you from the bottom of my heart:

Thank God. Above all I give thanks to my Lord and Savior, Jesus Christ, for the strength to turn the object of my pain into the subject of my success. All I am I give to you.

Leslie P. Graham-Wilson: I thank you for being the first to believe in my story. You gave me a chance to share it with others. I love and appreciate your counsel and support.

Pastor Falene S. Best: I thank you for being a listening ear when I needed one; I know it wasn't easy for you. I pray that God will continue to keep you and your family in perfect peace.

My little sister Cherell: Words can never describe my gratitude for always opening your heart and your home to me. I am so proud of you, and I continue to push myself to higher heights so that nothing will seem impossible for you. You are my inside out. I love you.

To my brother-in-law, thanks for the food, shelter, electricity, and so much more...LOL. You didn't have to do it, but you did.

My siblings: Without you all, I would have no reason to push. We are breaking generational curses one day at a time. I love you all.

To my Mother: Thank you for giving me life, love, and tough skin...LOL. I never wanted you to be perfect; I just wanted you to be happy. And I hope in some ways I made that possible.

To my pastor, Pastor Darrin Monroe: Thank you for helping me to believe that there are still honorable men of God out there who can be trusted to feed their sheep. It is a privilege to be a part of your congregation.

To Terry McMillan, Brenda Browder and Fran Drescher: I wanted to thank you all for publicly telling your unique stories of life with a homosexual man; I applaud you for your dignity, style, and grace, showing me that we are women worth celebrating. I pray nothing but love and happiness for you all. I look forward to meeting you all someday.

To every man I have ever loved, good and bad: Thanks for everything. I mean that sincerely.

To my agent, editor, publisher, and all those involved in bringing the vision to life, I thank you.

To my miracle workers (stylist, makeup artist, road manager, and personal assistant): You know who you are and if you don't, you'll find out...LOL. I couldn't do what I do without you.

To my ex-husband: The devil almost caused us to hate each other and keep each other bound by bitterness, but it didn't work. I Love you, and I know there is a work for you; God is not done with you yet. Be blessed.

Last, but not least, I send out a very special thanks to every person who purchased my book. I hope you were blessed by my testimony. I pray a special blessing finds you right where you are. Amen.

If you or someone you know is struggling emotionally as a result of losing a mate to a homosexual lifestyle, visit

W.H.Y.
Women of Homosexual Yokes
www.why4give.com
1(800)376-9091
A nonprofit organization located in the
Jersey City, NJ area

Also by visiting shaminallen.com

You can view the author's Up close and personal interview entitled: Becoming Transparent.

You will also find other empowering DVDs by Shamina Allen.

Stay tuned for upcoming motivational books by Shamina Allen

Until then enjoy excerpts from the next book entitled walking on water!

Walking On Water

Inspirational words to keep you afloat

Original Quotes and Sayings by Shamina Allen as well as scriptures and prayers designed to keep your eyes on God and not on circumstance

By Shamina Allen

Contents

Live

The thief cometh not, but for to steal, and to kill, and to destroy: I have come that they might have life, and that they might have it more abundantly.

– John 10:10

During your walk with God you will come to learn that giving up is not always a sign of defeat, but rather a demonstration of obedience.

If God were to hand deliver a package to you baring all your hearts desire, would you be available to receive it; would your hands be clean enough to open it and your heart soft enough to appreciate it. Position yourself to be blessed

The most expensive thing in this world is Pride.

Patience is the root of love, without it love will never survive.

Help is assisting, not taking over someone else's troubles, when help is used properly it creates a joy that words can't describe, but when used out of content it can give birth to bitter resentment

Worry is slavery of the mind.

Being anointed doesn't make you immune to life,
just effective in it.

Why do we pray for miracles and when we see it we can't
believe it? Why is it that we pray for the truth and when
we receive it we call it a lie? So instantly, by the power of
our Words, blessing, in our lives and others turn into curses
by our lack of faith and understanding. Sometimes, if it
seems too good to be true, it might be God.

We all want to experience the blessings & favor of Christ,
but we are not willing to use his methods. Humble yourself
to be blessed.

Sometimes taking two steps back in the natural really means advancing to another level in the spiritual. In this season the uncommon blessing requires uncommon sacrifice

The saddest thing I have ever seen was a person chasing their dreams outside of Gods will.

Love

If I have the gift of prophecy and can fathom all mysteries and all knowledge... but have not love, I am nothing
-1 Corinthians 13:2 (NIV)

Love waits for no man; it refuses to be bound by convenience or circumstance, it is the only thing in this world that can't be controlled.

True love never subtracts it only adds and multiples

Moving on can hurt, but staying still can be deadly. We all deserve to be in relationships where we feel appreciated and loved, if that is not the case, you don't need me to tell you what you already know, when it's your time to move on let it go gracefully.

Rushing leads to regret; always take time to think

To be in love is to experience complete harmony between the Mind, body and soul.

A City set on a Hill can not be hidden … I see you.

The greatest gift one can give is Love, but the greatest gift one can receive is destiny, the assurance of knowing that you have purpose in Gods divine plan, after all, what is life without purpose?

Sex and love are like life and death you can't fully appreciate one with out the other

Love is like olive oil it restores anything it touches.

I pray that your life is filled with love and happiness.

Learn

"Teach me good discernment and knowledge, for I believe in your commandments."   -Psalms 119:66

If you want to know the depths of a person look at their friends

Riding on someone else's accomplishments is like viewing Jesus with your eyes closed, you can never experience the true glory

A person that is loud is not necessarily heard

Something's are better left unsaid but deeply felt

A man with no integrity lives a life of hand to mouth, his family struggles and his house is cursed; but a man of honor is blessed and many give to his house without cause his family is blessed in and out of season.

A liar will never believe the truth

Beware of those that preach from the depths of the valley concerning how to make it up the mountain

There are weeds in every garden and thorns on every rose,

repent daily No man is perfect.

"I forgive you" doesn't mean I will pretend it never happened, it means I love God more then I dislike you, so I willingly give up my right to retaliate and I trade in my resentment for peace of mind

Excuses are wasted words that could be used to shape your future. Speak only those things worth seeing

The pen of a chosen author writes miracles in every line. Their vision changes lives and their steps our ordered. The chosen writer realizes that they don't just write books they are books living breathing words in motion.

We are living in a time where there are too many teachers and not enough students.

Discernment is as essential to your survival as breathing

Parenthood is not a reward; but a test from God.

Jealously is a disease that is highly contagious.

True knowledge is achieved through experience

I pray your strength as you learn the lessons of life.

Encourage

Anxiety in a man's heart weighs it down, but an encouraging word makes it glad.   -Proverbs 12:25

Sing, O barren, thou that didst not bear; break forth into singing, and cry aloud, thou that didst not travail with child: for more are the children of the desolate than the children of the married wife, saith the LORD.- Isaiah 54: 1

In a world where so many people have the same idea or similar agenda's its hard to believe that you can make a difference, but we must remember Matthew 22:14 For many are called, but few are chosen. This is the season for the chosen, so stay focused. Don't look behind you or around you because it doesn't matter.

An apple and an orange will never grow on the same tree; surround yourself by individuals with like goals

In this season those of us called to work must understand that the Devil knows he can't stop the visions, the creativity and the opportunities that God has for you, so his efforts are to make it impossible for you to work, by way of fatigue, sickness and stress. In the mist of working to fulfill your purpose remember to manage your flesh, don't forget to take a deep breath and rest, for our mission is heavenly; but our bodies are subjected to the earth, pace yourself.

I learned that when God wants to bless you he must first remove individuals from your life that are not worthy of experiencing your favor, Loss is an indictor of great things to come.

There is no failure in God; everything has a divine purpose in your life and contributes to your mental physical and emotional success.

Successful people are not afraid to learn.

You can only give what you have.

A squirrel will never fly to the top of a tree, but it can climb; except who you are and what you can do, and then- do it

It's amazing what God will do for you when you are

willing to do anything for him. Ask yourself how bad
do you want it?

If you want to see a miracle, look in the mirror

If you have to question whether or not a person should be
in your life, chances are they shouldn't

When I was a little girl I dreamt about the kind of woman I
would be when I got older, when I was a
teenager I dreamt about the kind of woman I would be
when I got my first job and a little bit of money in my
pocket, and as an adult I find myself dreaming about the
woman I would be if only I had the desires of my heart.
If you're anything like me, I think it's time we wake up,
stop dreaming and start living.

*I pray that you are successful in your life's work,
that you never yield to defeat and that you always lean
on God and not man*

CPSIA information can be obtained at www.ICGtesting.com
Printed in the USA
BVOW08s1102270916

463408BV00001B/9/P